The Berlin Wall

The Berlin Wall

Other books in the At Issue in History series:

The Assassination of John F. Kennedy
The Attack on Pearl Harbor
The Battle of Gettysburg
The Bay of Pigs
The Bill of Rights
The Civil Rights Act of 1964
The Conquest of the New World
The Crash of 1929
The Cuban Missile Crisis
Custer's Last Stand
The Declaration of Independence
The Discovery of the AIDS Virus
The Founding of the State of Israel
The Indian Reservation System
Japanese American Internment Camps
The McCarthy Hearings
The Nuremberg Trials
The Outbreak of the Civil War
Prohibition
Reconstruction
The Rise and Fall of the Taliban
The Rise of Adolf Hitler
The Salem Witch Trials
The Sinking of the Titanic
The Tiananmen Square Massacre
The Treaty of Versailles
The Waco Standoff

The Berlin Wall

Cindy Mur, *Book Editor*

Daniel Leone, *President*
Bonnie Szumski, *Publisher*
Scott Barbour, *Managing Editor*

OPPOSING
VIEWPOINTS® **AT ISSUE IN HISTORY**
SERIES

**GREENHAVEN
PRESS®**

THOMSON
———✳———™
GALE

San Diego • Detroit • New York • San Francisco • Cleveland
New Haven, Conn. • Waterville, Maine • London • Munich

For more information, contact
Greenhaven Press
27500 Drake Rd.
Farmington Hills, MI 48331-3535
Or you can visit our Internet site at http://www.gale.com

LIBRARY OF CONGRESS CATALOGING-IN-PUBLICATION DATA

The Berlin Wall / Cindy Mur, book editor.
    p. cm. — (At issue in history)
Includes bibliographical references and index.
ISBN 0-7377-1350-X (lib. : alk. paper) — ISBN 0-7377-1351-8 (pbk. : alk. paper)
    1. Berlin Wall, Berlin, Germany, 1961–1989. 2. Berlin (Germany)—Politics and
government—1945–1990. 3. Germany (East)—Social conditions. 4. Germany—
History—Unification, 1990. 5. Germany (East)—Politics and government—
1989–1990. 6. Opposition (Political science)—Germany (East)—History. I. Mur,
Cindy. II. Series.
DD881.B4766 2004
943.087—dc21   2003044857

Printed in the United States of America

Contents

Foreword   10

Introduction: The Rise and Fall of the Berlin Wall   12

Chapter 1: The Berlin Crisis

1. The Berlin Crisis Occurred Because Berlin Was
a Symbol of the Cold War *by Campbell Craig*   24
Soviet officials disliked the presence of Western
capitalism in the midst of Socialist East Germany; however, the West refused to abandon its
German allies. This standoff produced a rivalry
between East and West in Berlin.

2. The Berlin Crisis Occurred Because Berlin Was
of Vital Strategic Importance *by Paul Du Quenoy*   30
Because of Stalin's goal to expand Soviet influence and Khrushchev's desire to make East Germany a showplace of Socialist ideals, Berlin
became politically strategic for the Soviet Union.
NATO's presence in the city was a thorn in the
Soviet plan, causing heightened tensions between
the East and West.

3. The West Is Committed to Berlin
by John F. Kennedy   37
The thirty-fifth president of the United States
outlines his plans for protecting West Berlin
from Soviet occupation.

4. The East Will Not Withdraw from Berlin
by Nikita S. Khrushchev   49
The Soviet premier, speaking at a conference of
Eastern European leaders, responds to President
Kennedy's commitment to West Berlin.

Chapter 2: The Construction of the Berlin Wall

1. The Wall Was a Result of Tensions Between
the Soviet Union and East Germany
by Hope M. Harrison   55
The primary impetus for the construction of the

Berlin Wall lies in the relationship between the Soviet Union and East German officials. Walter Ulbricht's policies in East Germany promoted a mass exodus from there that left Soviet leader Nikita Khrushchev with no choice but to allow the construction of the Berlin Wall.

2. Western Response to the Construction of the Berlin Wall Was Appropriate *by Eric Morris*   70
Initially caught off guard, Western leaders showed restraint when the Berlin Wall went up. Any action in response to the construction of the wall could have provoked a nuclear war between the West and the Soviet Union.

3. The Construction of the Wall Alleviated East-West Tensions *by Richard Reeves*   84
The threat of a nuclear war between the United States and the Soviet Union was avoided when Soviet leader Nikita Khrushchev supported the creation of a wall dividing Berlin. The wall's presence allowed both sides to back away from a struggle over what to do with the Berlin crisis.

Chapter 3: The Fall of the Berlin Wall and the Consequences for Berlin

1. Berliners Celebrate the Destruction of the Berlin Wall *by Andreas Ramos*   88
Joyous celebration and chaos filled the streets of Berlin after the fall of the Berlin Wall.

2. The Fall of the Berlin Wall Creates Confusion and Euphoria for Berliners *by Christopher Hope*   96
After the wall came down, a new Berlin emerged—one characterized by both happiness and uncertainty.

3. The Economic Outlook Is Bright for Berlin *by Andrew J. Glass*   104
The economic outlook for Berlin is positive with new construction and the introduction of high technology industries to the city.

4. Economic and Social Difficulties Plague Berlin *by Belinda Cooper*   112
Problematic social, political, and economic con-

ditions after the fall of the wall have left Berlin facing many challenges as it becomes part of the European community.

Chronology   127

For Further Research   130

Index   136

Foreword

Historian Robert Weiss defines history simply as "a record and interpretation of past events." Both elements—record and interpretation—are necessary, Weiss argues.

Names, dates, places, and events are the essence of history. But historical writing is not a compendium of facts. It consists of facts placed in a sequence to tell a connected story. A work of history is not merely a story, however. It also must analyze what happened and *why*—that is, it must interpret the past for the reader.

For example, the events of December 7, 1941, that led President Franklin D. Roosevelt to call it "a date which will live in infamy" are fairly well known and straightforward. A force of Japanese planes and submarines launched a torpedo and bombing attack on American military targets in Pearl Harbor, Hawaii. The surprise assault sank five battleships, disabled or sank fourteen additional ships, and left almost twenty-four hundred American soldiers and sailors dead. On the following day, the United States formally entered World War II when Congress declared war on Japan.

These facts and consequences were almost immediately communicated to the American people who heard reports about Pearl Harbor and President Roosevelt's response on the radio. All realized that this was an important and pivotal event in American and world history. Yet the news from Pearl Harbor raised many unanswered questions. Why did Japan decide to launch such an offensive? Why were the attackers so successful in catching America by surprise? What did the attack reveal about the two nations, their people, and their leadership? What were its causes, and what were its effects? Political leaders, academic historians, and students look to learn the basic facts of historical events and to read the intepretations of these events by many different sources, both primary and secondary, in order to develop a more complete picture of the event in a historical context.

In the case of Pearl Harbor, several important questions surrounding the event remain in dispute, most notably the role of President Roosevelt. Some historians have blamed his policies for deliberately provoking Japan to attack in order to propel America into World War II; a few have gone so far as to accuse him of knowing of the impending attack but not informing others. Other historians, examining the same event, have exonerated the president of such charges, arguing that the historical evidence does not support such a theory.

The Greenhaven At Issue in History series recognizes that many important historical events have been interpreted differently and in some cases remain shrouded in controversy. Each volume features a collection of articles that focus on a topic that has sparked controversy among eyewitnesses, contemporary observers, and historians. An introductory essay sets the stage for each topic by presenting background and context. Several chapters then examine different facets of the subject at hand with readings chosen for their diversity of opinion. Each selection is preceded by a summary of the author's main points and conclusions. A bibliography is included for those students interested in pursuing further research. An annotated table of contents and thorough index help readers to quickly locate material of interest. Taken together, the contents of each of the volumes in the Greenhaven At Issue in History series will help students become more discriminating and thoughtful readers of history.

Introduction: The Rise and Fall of the Berlin Wall

In her book *Berlin: The Wall Is Not Forever*, Eleanor Lansing Dulles describes what was once East Germany's military stronghold along the border between East and West Berlin:

> Troops, variously estimated, but probably 30,000 in number, man 193 watch towers, 208 bunkers, and other reinforced positions. The patrols on the sector border are always in pairs to lessen the likelihood of their own escapes, and they have orders to shoot unauthorized persons at sight. It is estimated that the wall within the city is more than twenty-eight miles long, and the barrier surrounding the Western sectors of Berlin is more than seventy miles long. At most places the wall is between nine and twelve feet high. At the wider crossing points there are staggered concrete implacements to prevent a car or truck from gaining momentum to crash the wall and permit a precarious attempt to escape.[1]

What factors led to the 1961 construction and the twenty-eight-year preservation of such a gruesome divide? The origin for this division began sixteen years earlier at the end of World War II, with tensions escalating through the years between a democratic United States and a Communist Soviet Union.

In 1945, at the end of World War II, the United States and the other Allied powers—France, Great Britain, and the Union of Soviet Socialist Republics (USSR)—planned to occupy and govern conquered Germany. The garrisoning of Germany was done to prevent it from implementing any further aggression toward its European neighbors. All Allied parties agreed to divide Germany and its capital, Berlin, into four separate zones, West Germany and West

Berlin (called the Federal Republic of Germany) controlled by France, Great Britain, and the United States; and East Germany and East Berlin (called the German Democratic Republic) controlled by the USSR. Since the city of Berlin was located within the Soviet-controlled portion of the German state, West Berlin remained a democratic island surrounded by Communist forces.

By 1947 it was clear that the Western Allies—the United States, France, and Great Britain—were eager to return Germany to its sovereign rule. The Marshall Plan, presented in a speech on June 5, 1947, by the U.S. secretary of state, George C. Marshall, suggested Western support for the rebuilding of Europe by supplying food and other products. President Harry S. Truman agreed with Marshall that an economically recovered Europe would be more politically stable and would be unlikely to turn Communist. The Soviets were just as determined to hold on to their half of Germany and the rest of the Eastern European nations reclaimed from German armies during World War II. Russian dictator Joseph Stalin, fearful of Western aggression and obsessed over Russian safety, believed the Marshall Plan was presented to marginalize his own Communist ideology. He wanted Communist puppet leaders in all Soviet satellite nations—including Germany—to maintain a buffer zone between the West and the heart of the USSR. The conflict in plans for the future of Germany added to the already growing suspicion and distrust between the Soviet Union and the American-led Western alliance.

Thus began the rivalry and mistrust called the Cold War between the democratic Allies led by President Truman and the Communist Soviet Union controlled by Stalin. In 1946 Winston Churchill, the former prime minister of Great Britain, stated that an "iron curtain" had fallen across Europe.

The first increase in tensions between the United States and the Soviet Union occurred on June 24, 1948. Until this date, all commerce and transportation to and from West Berlin was done through East Germany. The Soviets decided to block access into West Berlin in response to an introduction of currency reform there without Soviet consent. The Western Allies reacted by airlifting a total of 2.3 million tons of food and supplies so the citizens of West Berlin could survive during the blockade. The airlifts continued until May 12, 1949, when the Soviets reopened the East German borders for transportation, realizing that the blockade had failed.

During this time, the Western Allies were forming a new alliance called the North Atlantic Treaty Organization (NATO). This organization was political and military in nature, designed to halt aggression or resist attack directed against any alliance member. The treaty forming the organization was signed on April 4, 1949, and its initial members included Belgium, Canada, Denmark, France, Iceland, Italy, Luxembourg, the Netherlands, Norway, Portugal, the United Kingdom, and the United States. With Soviet-dominated nations conspicuously absent, it was obvious that Russia was considered the potential aggressor that NATO would repel in the event the Cold War turned hot.

Germany, now the border between East and West, suffered under the dread of open war. Tensions between the newly allied NATO nations and the Soviets were heightened in the summer of 1952, when the border between East and West Germany was closed, except for the section that separated Berlin. East Germans were especially distraught, for now they could not leave their Communist-controlled state if they wanted. After a year, on June 17, 1953, East Germans protested vigorously in the streets against the political and economic policies of their Communist government. Their protests were quelled by the Soviet Union, which sent in tanks to enforce peace in the area. The border between East and West Germany remained closed.

Joseph Stalin died in 1953 and Nikita Khrushchev took his place as leader of the Soviet Union after a brief power struggle within the Communist Party. Stalin had been a proponent of a unified Germany, even one not under Communist control, if he were to gain some strategic advantage in doing so. Khrushchev did not adhere to that belief and instead considered a non-Socialist East Germany as an ideological loss he could not afford. With its comparatively strong economy, Khrushchev was determined to make East Germany a showpiece of Socialist success. But the divided Berlin left Western influence pricking like a thorn in the side of his model state.

In 1955 Khrushchev began to make Berlin the central wheel upon which all his negotiations with the West revolved. According to Eric Morris in his book *Blockade: Berlin and the Cold War,* "For Khrushchev, West Berlin symbolized the threat to the Soviet empire in Eastern Europe."[2] He needed a way to show—if not by example then by force—that Soviet ideology would prevail no matter what the will of East Europeans. When West Germany joined NATO in 1955, Khrushchev responded by forming his own organization, describing it as a defensive measure. On May 15, 1955, Moscow, along with the puppet governments of seven other Eastern European satellites, signed the Warsaw Pact. This arrangement strengthened the Soviets' position both in military and political terms. The Soviets demonstrated their oppressive might in Hungary by militarily suppressing a rebellion there against communism in 1956.

Although the Soviets controlled East Germany, one individual, Walter Ulbricht, began to influence the policies the Soviets implemented there. Since 1946 Ulbricht had been chairman and secretary-general of the Socialist Unity Party in the German Democratic Republic (GDR). In this position, he tried to convince Khrushchev to take control of all of Berlin. He thought this would increase his own power in the region. In 1958 Khrushchev began to listen more attentively to Ulbricht, who stated that "all of Berlin lies in the territory of the GDR" and that the allies had no basis for occupying it. On November 27, 1958, Khrushchev issued an ultimatum demanding that West Berlin become a "demilitarized free city," meaning that all Western troops leave within six months. The Western allies, led by U.S. president Dwight D. Eisenhower, ignored Khrushchev's demand. According to historian Paul Du Quenoy, "Recently released evidence shows that President Eisenhower almost certainly knew that Khrushchev's bluster about Soviet superiority in nuclear-missile technology was a bluff."[3] Therefore, Khrushchev's attempt to oust the allies from Berlin, despite the threat of a nuclear war, failed to budge Western occupation. When his six-month deadline passed, Khrushchev did nothing in response. The threat was hollow, and so the NATO allies remained in Berlin. However, Khrushchev's demand had succeeded in increasing tension between the East and the West yet again, forcing NATO to consider the very real possibility of a nuclear war.

Until this time, the United States had always maintained a military superiority over the Soviet Union because of its nuclear capabilities. But by the late 1950s the Soviet Union was rumored to have attained a comparable level of nuclear weaponry. How to handle the threat of nuclear war was the most critical problem that John F. Kennedy faced when he became president of the United States in 1961. He promised to take a firm stand against the spread of communism.

Only four months into his presidency, in April 1961, Kennedy trained fifteen hundred Cuban exiles to return to their homeland and oust its self-appointed Communist leader, Fidel Castro. The invasion failed miserably, and the resulting fiasco led Khrushchev to believe that Kennedy was a weak leader. As a result, Khrushchev renewed his 1958 ultimatum for the NATO allies to abandon West Berlin. Despite his pledge to respond more firmly to the

Soviets, Kennedy reacted as Eisenhower had before him: He refused to take a hard line. While the leadership of the United States was considering how to respond to Khrushchev's ultimatum without bringing about a nuclear war or appearing weak, Khrushchev soon provided the solution that would allow the Western leaders to escape the trap of their own indecisiveness.

In East Germany Walter Ulbricht had not given up his insistence to Khrushchev that Berlin should be one city. He wanted all of Berlin for East Germany primarily because of the mass exodus of people leaving the East for the West through Berlin. Ulbricht's Communist policies had alienated East Germans, primarily young people and many educated professionals: doctors, engineers, and professors. These refugees fled to freedom in West Berlin. Ulbricht believed that by claiming all of Berlin, he would stop the tide of refugees, numbering in the hundreds of thousands per year. After Khrushchev's unsuccessful 1961 ultimatum to relinquish West Berlin, the number of refugees increased to more than 1,000 per day. From January to August 1961 the flow almost doubled to 207,000 people. Because Khrushchev wanted to maintain control of East Germany, Ulbricht still had the necessary leverage to promote his own policies.

Therefore, in the summer of 1961 Ulbricht succeeded in persuading Khrushchev that the only way to stop the huge exodus was to use force—to build a wall. On August 13, 1961, in the early hours of a Sunday morning, East German soldiers and workmen began to separate East and West Berlin. Ulbricht called it an "antifascist wall of protection," yet its primary purpose was to keep East German citizens from leaving.

Burkhard Kirste, a lecturer at the Freie Universitat Berlin, describes the events of the early morning blockade:

> Early in the morning of Sunday, August 13, 1961, the GDR began under the leadership of [East German leader] Erich Honecker to block off East Berlin and the GDR from West Berlin by means of barbed wire and antitank obstacles. Streets were torn up, and barricades of paving stones were erected. Tanks gathered at crucial places. The subway and local railway services between East and West Berlin were interrupted. Inhabitants of East Berlin and the GDR were no longer

allowed to enter West Berlin, amongst them 60,000 commuters who had worked in West Berlin so far. In the following days, construction brigades began replacing the provisional barriers by a solid wall.[4]

There has been much speculation as to what President Kennedy knew or did not know about the possibility of the wall's construction. Kennedy was vacationing in Hyannis Port that weekend and did not return to Washington until Monday, even though he had been informed that the barrier was being built. Once he returned to Washington, the president did not publicly act until five days following the wall's construction. On August 18 he sent about fifteen hundred soldiers to reinforce the military presence already in Berlin. The move was not particularly threatening, and the Soviets shrugged it off.

Some assert that Kennedy and his administration were caught unaware, which explains why they took no action to prevent the wall from going up. Berlin was a vibrant city, and few expected the East to close it off. Some in the administration have stated that they expected a citizens' uprising following the large emigration, not a crackdown by East German officials. One American commander in Berlin, General Watson, was quoted in 1967 as saying, "We expected at the time that the East Germans would try to control the refugee outflow, but no one expected a wall."[5] In addition, some officials did not believe that the East would make such a bold move since it might receive retaliation from the West.

Others think that Kennedy must have known that the wall was a real possibility. The administration was well aware of the massive flight from East Germany and that the East would probably act to stop it. Kennedy was heard to say that he knew Khrushchev was in an untenable position with East Germany's refugee problem, stating, "The entire East bloc is in danger. He has to do something to stop this. Perhaps a wall."[6] It seems unlikely, therefore, that the Berlin Wall came as a complete surprise.

Historian Campbell Craig discusses Kennedy's response to the creation of the wall:

> While publicly expressing outrage, Kennedy and his advisers privately breathed a sigh of relief. Not one major official in the White House advocated a military challenge to the wall. . . . The wall put an end to the

struggle between the United States and the Soviet Union over the status of Berlin: it remained an artificially divided city, a cold-war peculiarity.[7]

This may ultimately help to clarify the reasons for erecting the Berlin Wall and why the wall remained in place for so many years. Its existence succeeded in reducing tensions between powerful countries that had the capacity to annihilate each other many times over.

This was by no means the end of the Cold War between the United States and the USSR. Other events occurred in which tensions rose between them again: the Cuban Missile Crisis, the Vietnam War, and the invasion of Czechoslovakia are a few.

As these events between East and West played out on an international level during the years the Berlin Wall was in place, the citizens of East Berlin were held under Communist rule, now prevented from crossing the border into West Berlin. In its first weeks the wall was primarily just barbed wire, and many people were able to sneak through it. One East Berliner who escaped over the wall was Conrad Schumann. Schumann was posted as a guard along the wall on August 15, 1961, just a few days after the wall was erected. He narrated his story in 1989, after the wall fell:

> I was thinking about how beautiful West Berlin was, and then I thought about the arms buildup that was going on in the East. I had seen the Russians and their tanks. The situation seemed to be growing more dangerous by the hour. I stood there for two hours, looking toward West Berlin and looking back at East Berlin. Then I jumped.[8]

Schumann's leap became an inspiration for the many East Berliners who attempted to follow him to West Berlin. More than five thousand people managed to escape either through or over the wall during the years of its existence. Some West Berliners risked their lives to establish an underground system, smuggling East Berliners across in cars with hiding places or by providing them with forged papers.

Not all those who attempted escape succeeded. One especially tragic death was that of eighteen-year-old Peter Fechter. Journalist Timothy W. Ryback relates the details of Fechter's escape effort:

Fechter had climbed through the barbed wire and was scrambling for the Wall before East German guards caught sight of him. Escaping a hail of machine-gun fire, Fechter reached the Wall and pulled himself to the top. Just as he was about to leap across, two bullets ripped into his back and a third into his stomach. He balanced for an instant atop the Wall before collapsing back into the Eastern sector. For the next fifty minutes Fechter lay at the base of the Wall, less than a yard from West Berlin, begging for assistance. Berliners from both East and West listened, and East Berliners watched, as the young man slowly bled to death.[9]

Until the destruction of the wall, crosses dotted the concrete edifice as memorials to the lives lost trying to cross the border. All told, over 260 people died attempting to go over the Berlin Wall.

It is not hard, then, to imagine the joy felt by Berliners on both sides of the wall when it began to come down. Ironically, the circumstances surrounding the opening of the wall on November 9, 1989, were initiated by an error made by a GDR official. Gunter Schabowski, a government spokesman, had just finished a press conference and, in shuffling through some papers, read that the government would now allow "all citizens to leave the country through the official border crossing points."[10] Actually, Schabowski had no authorization to read that statement, and he did not read it in its entirety: Travel was supposed to be dependent on the strict issuance of visas. The damage was done, however. The local television station reported his remarks, and word quickly spread that East Berlin citizens were free to go across the border into West Berlin.

Within the hour, East Berliners began to gather at the wall's checkpoints. At first, the guards rebuffed any requests to cross, but they eventually began letting people through, perhaps after hearing the news themselves. Excited East Berliners, some dressed in bedclothes and slippers with coats thrown over them, rushed to the wall. Once the news spread in the West, West Berliners hurried to welcome the East Berliners as they came through. One historian describes the scene:

> The cheers rose, the singing mounted to a crescendo—
> old Berlin ditties, new pop songs, the national anthem,

the Lutheran hymn "Nun Danket alle Gott" ["Now Thank We All Our God"]. The crowds banged on the car roofs, reached inside to shake hands or thrust flowers and wine bottles at the occupants. They sprayed everything with champagne and kissed everyone within reach.[11]

The celebrating continued through the night and into the next day. Whole sections of the Berlin Wall began to be demolished. Once on the other side, East Berliners gazed in amazement at the bounty they saw available in the West, products they had been denied for twenty-eight years: fresh produce, fine chocolates, perfumed soaps, stylish shoes. For many, it was a time of reuniting with family members. Hundreds had not seen each other since the wall went up in 1961. Grandchildren had been born and were being met for the first time.

A study of the years since the fall of the wall reveals that reunification has not been an easy time for East and West Berliners as they have had to overcome many obstacles, both economic and sociological. But during those early days in November 1989, there was great happiness. The Berlin Wall had finally come down.

Notes

1. Eleanor Lansing Dulles, *Berlin: The Wall Is Not Forever.* Chapel Hill: University of North Carolina Press, 1967, p. 47.
2. Eric Morris, *Blockade: Berlin and the Cold War.* London: Hamish Hamilton, 1973, p. 195.
3. Paul Du Quenoy, "Berlin Crises," *History in Dispute*, vol. 1, *The Cold War*, ed. Benjamin Frankel. Detroit: St. James, 1999.
4. Burkhard Kirste, *The Berlin Wall*, February 26, 2003. www.userpage.chemie.fu-berlin.de.
5. Quoted in Eleanor Lansing Dulles, *The Wall: A Tragedy in Three Acts.* Columbia: Institute of International Studies, University of South Carolina, 1972, pp. 27–28.
6. Quoted in Richard Reeves, "How the Wall Prevented World War 3," *The Star-Ledger* (Newark, NJ), November 15, 1999, p. 15.
7. Campbell Craig, "Berlin Crises," *History in Dispute*,

vol. 1, *The Cold War*, ed. Benjamin Frankel. Detroit: St. James, 1999.

8. Quoted in Michael Ryan, "A New Day in Berlin," *People Weekly*, December 4, 1989, p. 70.

9. Timothy W. Ryback, "Why the Wall Still Stands," *Atlantic*, August 1986, pp. 20–25.

10. Ann Tusa, *The Last Division: A History of Berlin, 1945–1989*. Reading, MA: Addison-Wesley, 1997, p. 370.

11. Tusa, *The Last Division*, p. 373.

Chapter 1

The Berlin Crisis

1

The Berlin Crisis Occurred Because Berlin Was a Symbol of the Cold War

Campbell Craig

In this selection, Campbell Craig states that Berlin's symbolic significance to capitalist and Communist forces during the Cold War brought about the Berlin crisis. In particular, Berlin was at the center of a growing "military and political rivalry between the United States and the Soviet Union over central Europe" from the end of World War II until the Berlin Wall was built in 1961. Soviet officials disliked the idea of a capitalist presence in the middle of Communist-controlled East Germany and demanded the West's departure from Berlin. Western powers refused to abandon West Berliners, and initially their position was supported by the superior nuclear capabilities of the United States.

By the late 1950s, however, the Soviet Union had the same military resources, and the Soviets renewed their ultimatums for Western departure. The West tried negotiating with the Soviets, but no plan was agreed upon. The Soviet leadership decided to build the Berlin Wall to remove the temptation of Western life from East German citizens. They then withdrew their demand for the Western powers to leave Berlin, and tensions eased between East and West. Campbell Craig is a lecturer in the history department at the University of Canterbury in New Zealand.

Campbell Craig, "Berlin Crises," *History in Dispute*, volume 1, *The Cold War*, edited by Benjamin Frankel. Farmington Hills, MI: St. James Press, 1999. Copyright © 1999 by St. James Press. Reproduced by permission of The Gale Group.

The Prussian city of Berlin, the capital city of Germany during the Third Reich, was one of the most profound symbols of the cold war. The occupation of Berlin by American, French, British, and Soviet troops for four decades after the Second World War reminded the world of the military and political foundations of the cold war. Berlin was the only place in Europe where American and Russian forces faced one another directly, for they were separated elsewhere on the continent by the buffer of central Europe. While troops confronted one another at the Checkpoint Charlie and Friedrichstrasse border crossings, Berlin was also the center of high-level intrigue and espionage and of competing claims for the German political soul, with the imported glitz and prosperity of West Berlin contending with the grim and ostensibly egalitarian East Berlin. It was also the home of the infamous Berlin Wall. Its erection in 1961 demonstrated like nothing else an admission by the Soviet Union that their working-class paradise was failing— while its destruction in 1989 symbolized like nothing else the final collapse of the myth.

The significance of Berlin in the history of the cold war, however, lies not in its historical and ideological symbolism, as important as these were. Rather, Berlin's central role was as a direct stake in the military and political rivalry between the United States and the Soviet Union over central Europe. On three separate occasions—in 1948–1949, 1958–1959, and 1961—the superpowers pushed their squabble over control of the western sectors of Berlin into bona fide cold-war crises. The evolving status of Berlin from 1948 to 1961 represents quite accurately the growth of Soviet military power to the point of effective thermonuclear parity with the United States. This fact makes [Russian] Premier Nikita Khrushchev's decision to build the wall in 1961 a great irony of recent history.

The Struggle for Berlin

At the end of the Second World War, the four allies—Great Britain, France, the United States, and the Soviet Union— each occupied sectors of Berlin, as victorious nations often divide a vanquished nation's capital. Once the Second World War was over, the formal purposes of occupation were becoming distant memories, subsumed by the cold-war division of Germany into East and West. Berlin, in the

eastern German region of Prussia, rested well inside the
Soviet-held portion of Germany, which had also been divided into occupied regions. The cold war turned these
three former allies into enemies of the Soviets, and there
arose the peculiar situation of having American, British, and
French soldiers and diplomats ranging about a large city in
the middle of the Soviet bloc. Naturally, the Soviet Union
was eager to see the three Western nations leave Berlin.
During meetings of the Allied Control Council in 1947–
1948, the Soviet delegates demanded with increasing impatience that the Western powers pack up and leave.

*A departure by the West would demoralize
Western Europeans, making them feel that the
Americans would abandon them at the first sign
of trouble.*

Nevertheless, many in the West, particularly Americans
stationed in Berlin, as well as non- or anticommunist West
Berliners, argued that the Soviet demand should be re-
buffed. Secretary of State George C. Marshall emphasized
that the Western powers still had a legal right to remain in
Berlin, since a formal peace treaty ending the Second World
War had never been completed. Berliners such as Willy
Brandt, mayor of Berlin (1957–1966) and later chancellor of
West Germany (1969–1974), called attention to the plight
of two million West Berliners who would be consigned to
the Soviet bloc should the Western powers depart. Robert
D. Murphy, a State Department expert on Germany, and
General Lucius D. Clay, U.S. Army commander in Berlin,
provided the most compelling argument: a departure by the
West would demoralize Western Europeans, making them
feel that the Americans would abandon them at the first
sign of trouble. So after Soviet premier Joseph Stalin decided to raise the stakes by establishing a formal ground
blockade around Berlin in the summer of 1948, President
Harry S. Truman decided to contest it by airlifting supplies
to the isolated citizens during the winter of 1948–1949. The
heroic efforts of American and British airmen and the en-
durance of the citizens of West Berlin made the airlift a success. In early 1949 the Soviet Union gave up, abandoned its

blockade, and reconciled itself, for the time being, to a divided Berlin.

Though the moral obligation to the West Berliners and the fear of a "bandwagon effect" certainly influenced the American decision to stay, the basic reason the United States chose to remain in Berlin was because it could. At that moment the United States held a monopoly over the atomic bomb, making the Soviet Union extremely averse to pushing matters toward war over a stake such as Berlin. The Americans could afford to take a hard-line position on Berlin. They exploited this accident of history because the Soviets were not prepared to go to war. Even with the American "occupation" as aggravating as it was, the massive Red Army could not stop planes from dropping atomic bombs on Russian cities. The Americans perceived the Soviets' unwillingness and exploited the U.S. advantage.

The Threat of Nuclear War

As with so many other events and trends of the cold war, the gradual Soviet attainment of a thermonuclear arsenal in the late 1950s changed the dynamics of the debate over Berlin substantially. In November 1958, having put up with the Western occupation of West Berlin for thirteen years, Khrushchev issued an ultimatum: the Western powers would have to leave in six months. The continued occupation, he said aptly, was like "a bone in my throat." Now that the Soviet Union had thermonuclear bombs, Khrushchev believed, the determination of the West to stand tough over its Second World War occupation rights in Berlin would falter.

The wall put an end to the struggle between the United States and the Soviet Union over the status of Berlin.

Despite the official North Atlantic Treaty Organization (NATO) policy of refusing to negotiate while under an ultimatum and treating any Soviet move against West Berlin as an act of general war, the Western powers, led by President Dwight D. Eisenhower, scrambled to find some kind of compromise. The British in particular were aghast at the idea of initiating a thermonuclear world war over the political status of West Berlin. Eisenhower deftly played on these British fears, quietly going along with Prime Minister Harold Macmillan's plea for a four-power summit (despite the no-negotiation policy) and put off contingency plans for a war to defend Berlin. Khrushchev, despite his tough rhetoric, gladly seized the opportunity to negotiate. Delegates from all four powers met in Geneva in the spring of 1959. Khrushchev even visited the United States that fall and was prepared to finalize a compromise over Berlin with Eisenhower at the Paris summit in 1960 when the downing of an American U-2 spy plane in Soviet territory derailed the talks, leaving the Berlin question unresolved.

As many in the West predicted, Khrushchev revived his ultimatum once a new American president, John F. Kennedy, assumed office in January 1961. The failure of the U.S.-sponsored invasion of Cuba in April 1961 persuaded Khrushchev that Kennedy was weak, and at a June 1961 summit meeting in Vienna the Soviet leader delivered his ultimatum to Kennedy. The Kennedy administration thus had to confront the same issue that Eisenhower had: whether or not the United States should go to war to protect West Berlin.

The Berlin Wall Eases Tensions

Despite Kennedy's campaign rhetoric about waging a virile and dynamic cold war, the new administration, like the previous one, declined to take a hard line on Berlin. Realizing that the military policy left to them by Eisenhower allowed for little choice in a war over Berlin—street skirmishes or global thermonuclear exchange—Kennedy administration officials began to consider how to avoid actual conflict while at the same time appearing to give in to the ultimatum. Khrushchev, equally nervous about going to war over the issue, provided the answer: a wall around West Berlin. The wall would allow the Western powers to retain their formal occupying status, while stopping the exodus of East Germans and eliminating the temptation to East Germans of Western capitalist prosperity and glamour. Best of all, it would allow Khrushchev to cancel his ultimatum. In August of 1961 East German leader Walter Ulbricht, with Khrushchev's approval, ordered his soldiers to begin erecting a large wall around the western sectors of Berlin. This wall gradually developed into a formal cold-war boundary, replete with watchtowers, guard dogs, and barbed wire: a sad, unmistakable symbol of the unpopularity of Soviet communism.

While publicly expressing outrage, Kennedy and his advisers privately breathed a sigh of relief. Not one major official in the White House advocated a military challenge to the wall. When Lucius Clay, the newly appointed ambassador to the enclosed city of West Berlin, tried to start a war anyway in October, the White House was forced to reel him in. The wall put an end to the struggle between the United States and the Soviet Union over the status of Berlin: it remained an artificially divided city, a cold-war peculiarity (not unlike Korea) until the Soviet empire began to collapse in the late 1980s and Berliners knocked the structure down.

2

The Berlin Crisis Occurred Because Berlin Was of Vital Strategic Importance

Paul Du Quenoy

In the following viewpoint, Paul Du Quenoy states that the strategic political importance of Berlin to the United States and the Soviet Union brought about the Berlin crisis. Du Quenoy outlines the attempts by Soviet premier Joseph Stalin to expand Soviet influence throughout Eastern Europe. These attempts were met with opposition from the West; however, the Soviets succeeded in gaining control over all the Eastern European Communist countries.

In 1955, a new Soviet leader, Nikita S. Khrushchev, sought to demonstrate the superiority of socialism with a successful East German state. To do this, he had to prevent the loss of millions of East German citizens to West Germany through West Berlin. Thus, Khrushchev allowed the construction of the Berlin Wall to maintain political strength in East Germany. Paul Du Quenoy is a Ph.D. history candidate at Georgetown University and is coeditor of the *History in Dispute Encyclopedia: The Cold War.*

One provision of the wartime agreements among the four Allied powers provided for their joint post–Second World War occupation of Germany with a sharing

Paul Du Quenoy, "Berlin Crises," *History in Dispute*, volume 1, *The Cold War*, edited by Benjamin Frankel. Farmington Hills, MI: St. James Press, 1999. Copyright © 1999 by St. James Press. Reproduced by permission of The Gale Group.

of administrative authority. Although the city of Berlin was located well within the Soviet zone of occupation, it, too, was divided among the four allies. The onset of the cold war and loss of the wartime strategic partnership of the three Western allies with the Soviet Union meant that the future of Germany stood little chance of being decided by its mutually hostile occupiers. The future of Berlin was even more clouded.

The Cold War Develops

The crisis atmosphere that surrounded the city must be understood in the context of the developing Cold War. By 1946 Soviet premier Joseph Stalin, while trying to maintain a conciliatory relationship with the West, also followed his obsession with Soviet security and attempted to expand Soviet influence as far and wide as possible without drawing the West into a general war that the Soviet Union was in no condition to fight. As a result, in July 1946 Soviet foreign minister Vyacheslav Molotov demanded that the industrial Ruhr region, well inside the Western zones, be shared with the Soviet Union. There were no provisions for Soviet occupation there in the four allies' occupation agreement, and the attempt to justify the demand by saying that the USSR [Union of Soviet Socialist Republics] was not getting enough reparation from Germany was ill founded. Indeed, accounts of the Soviet military administration's transfer to Russia of almost all the heavy industrial base in its zone and its use of large numbers of the population for slave labor did not suggest to anyone that reparations were lacking. Rejecting the Soviet demand out of hand, the Western allies were becoming increasingly convinced that the USSR was an unreliable partner in joint occupation. Shortly thereafter, the three Western allies made plans to combine their zones politically and economically.

Further afield, Soviet attempts to extract military-base rights and territorial concessions from Turkey and Iran, two other places where no wartime agreement guaranteed the Soviets a future role, met with firm Western resistance. Although we now know that Stalin pressured Josip Tito, the leader of the Communist Party in Yugoslavia, not to arm or support the communist rebellion in Greece lest it provoke a Western military response, the West perceived that Moscow was behind the Greek uprising, and, in March 1947,

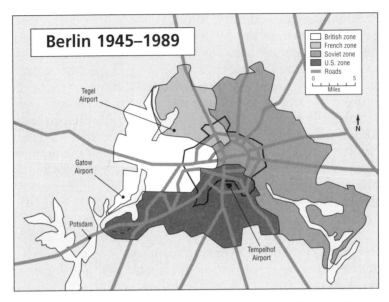

President Harry S. Truman elaborated the Truman Doctrine of U.S. resistance to communist expansion anywhere in the world. Irregularities in Soviet promises to allow democratic governments in eastern Europe also caused concern in the West.

When the announcement of the Marshall Plan in June 1947 caused Stalin to believe that the United States was trying to marginalize extreme ideologies, such as his own, throughout Europe, he used coercion to force the otherwise enthusiastic governments of eastern Europe to reject participation in the plan. Realizing that he had perhaps miscalculated what the West would tolerate, he moved to consolidate what already lay within his grasp. In September 1947 he reorganized the international communist movement into a Moscow-led organization, the Cominform, or Communist Information Bureau. Later that autumn he instructed east European communists to take control of their countries through extralegal means, a process that was completed by the following February when every east European state except Yugoslavia and Greece was governed by Moscow-directed communist regimes.

The German Question

Despite these provocative actions, it is apparent that Stalin still believed he could reach some sort of accommodation over the German question. Indeed, the East German Communist Party had been deliberately left out of the first Cominform meeting, while even the French and Italian communists sent delegates. For Stalin the best outcome for Germany would have been a unified state that was politically nonaligned and disarmed. Indeed, there was much thought even among West German politicians (such as the leading Social Democrat, Kurt Schumacher) that was favorable to this approach. It was also possible that the dramatic economic and social reforms undertaken by the Soviet military administration in its zone, all of which were communist in complexion, could potentially lead to the full communization of the unified country.

The Western allies were becoming increasingly convinced that the USSR was an unreliable partner in joint occupation.

Stalin had to find some way to stop the continued integration of the Western zones, a process started by Molotov's 1946 demand. The joint introduction of a reformed German currency in the Western sectors of Berlin was the immediate cause of Stalin's decision to declare a land and water blockade of the city in June 1948. He was creating a crisis over an anomalous feature of the occupation agreement in order to demonstrate his serious desire to promote a four-power solution to the German question (not a solution decided by three of the powers to his exclusion). In his strategic thinking the allies could either let West Berlin starve and fall under Russian control or come crawling to him for negotiations in which he would have the upper hand. Perhaps Stalin was also thinking about his own failure to prevent mass starvation during the siege of Leningrad. What he missed was that the West, especially the United States, had the capability and the will to risk aerial conflict and provide daily supplies of food, fuel, and consumer goods to a city of two million people for more than a year. The West carried out a tremendous feat. Its only alternative was to give in to Stalin either over Berlin or over Germany as a whole and look weak.

Stalin, however, was not fully estranged from a policy that would have resulted in German reunification. Even after the Western zones and the Soviet zone were made into two separate German states in 1949, East German officials were plagued by fears that Stalin would jettison their country if he could gain some strategic advantage by doing so. Indeed, the Soviet leader's "peace notes" on Germany, written in March 1952, proposed a scheme for German reunification according to which both German states would enter a confederative structure [an alliance] on equal footing, even though East Germany was about one third the size and had about one-third the population of the West. The Western allies did not accept the plan. In addition to its absurd equivalence of the two German states, the strategic disadvantage that losing West Germany's military and industrial potential was simply too great to countenance.

Khrushchev's Aggressive Approach

Stalin's death in March 1953 and other evolving features of the Cold War changed the situation without reducing the tension that surrounded West Berlin. In the power struggle that followed, Stalin's designated successor, Georgy Malenkov, and his associates followed a "New Course" of developing a broad domestic economic base and trying to relax international tensions. Other Soviet leaders, led by Nikita Khrushchev, attacked this policy as weak and even as a betrayal of socialism. By 1955 Malenkov and his new strategic approach, which reached back to what appeared to be Stalin's, were no longer factors in the Soviet government. Significantly, one of Malenkov's associates, secret police chief Lavrenty Beria, was executed after a not-quite-so-fair trial in which he was accused of conspiring to sell out East Germany to the West.

Khrushchev's confrontational approach was important for the city of Berlin and for Germany as a whole. By the 1950s the dynamics of the Soviets' relationship with their East German allies became skewed. When Khrushchev began his de-Stalinization campaign in February 1956, the East German leadership, under the Stalinist Walter Ulbricht, once again feared for its survival. Seeking to compete with the West in order to demonstrate the superiority of socialism, Khrushchev simply could not afford to let East Germany be subsumed into a reunified German state, regardless of whatever strategic value that solution might have had for Stalin. Allowing a socialist state to revert to something other than socialism was not acceptable in an ideological struggle. The East German economy, moreover, was by far the best in eastern Europe. (Its geographic history as an integral part of industrial Germany predisposed it to be.) Khrushchev believed East Germany would serve as a "display window" (Schaufenster) for socialism.

Keeping East Germany viable, however, was a terrible problem. While the borders of the occupation zones had been relatively free, millions of people simply left to assimilate into the socially and economically freer West Germany. When the borders were closed after East Germany became a separate state, the four-power presence in Berlin still allowed free transit to the West for any East German who took the Berlin subway into the Western sectors. As East German socialism continued to stifle initiative and personal liberty, hundreds of thousands of East Germans chose that way out.

Seeking to compete with the West in order to demonstrate the superiority of socialism, Khrushchev simply could not afford to let East Germany be subsumed into a reunified German state.

The loss of what were predominantly young, educated people to the West; the ruthless exploitation of the East German economy by the Soviet occupation; and Ulbricht's continuing Stalinist communization of society and the economy raised serious questions about his regime's ability to survive without significant help from the USSR. Recent research has revealed that Ulbricht had considerable leverage in the alliance relationship between the two countries; for Khrushchev could either support him to his complete satisfaction or let his state collapse. Demanding that the West evacuate Ulbricht's capitol in November 1958, Khrushchev was attempting to shore up his ally's legitimacy. (Having half one's capital city occupied by mortal enemies does raise questions of legitimacy.) He was also trying to employ what many believed to be the Soviet advantage in strategic weapons to make a major play for Soviet foreign policy.

Khrushchev's ploy did not work. Recently released evidence shows that President Eisenhower almost certainly knew that Khrushchev's bluster about Soviet superiority in nuclear-missile technology was a bluff. Intelligence reports about the problems of the Soviet strategic-weapons program and the complete lack of aerial-espionage evidence to sustain the Soviet leader's claims of superiority enabled the West to ignore him without suffering undue consequences over Berlin.

A Peaceful Solution

By mid 1959 Khrushchev was aware that his bid for strategic-weapons superiority was at an end and that the success of the American strategic-weapons program might well leave the Soviet Union at a disadvantage. The Soviet leader began to approach the West with what seemed to be a desire to relax tensions. After a successful visit to the United States in the fall of 1959, relations warmed for a time. The downing of an American spy plane over Soviet territory in April 1960, however, threw a wrench into a planned summit between Khrushchev and Eisenhower in Paris and caused the attempt at an early détente to founder.

Despite some efforts to renew the relationship with the Kennedy administration, which came into office in January 1961, the pressures of the East German alliance evolved into a major disruption. After a relatively unpromising meeting with Kennedy in Vienna in June 1961, it seemed apparent to Khrushchev that the best the Eastern bloc could hope for was a solution to the flight of East Germany's population. This problem became more pronounced in Soviet strategic thinking after Kennedy resisted attempts to lure him into firm American military commitments in Cuba and Laos. On 13 August 1961, with no real hope of dislodging the West from Berlin and the continuing exodus of East Germans for the West, the Soviet leader consented to the implementation of a plan code-named "Rose": building a wall around West Berlin. The stability crisis in East Germany was shored up, the battle lines of the Cold War were solidified, and the Berlin crisis was over.

3

The West Is Committed to Berlin

John F. Kennedy

On July 25, 1961, President John F. Kennedy addressed the American people regarding escalating tensions between the United States and the Soviet Union over Berlin. In his speech, Kennedy affirms that the United States will remain committed to West Berlin, as was its right through signed agreements with the Soviet Union. He outlines the steps that the United States will take to make good on that commitment and to abate a worldwide threat from communism. Kennedy asserts that the Berlin crisis is a test of Western courage and that the United States "must be ready to resist with force" if called upon. Therefore, a military build up of personnel and armaments is necessary. Despite this preparation for war, Kennedy pledges to seek peaceful solutions to this conflict with the Soviet Union.

Good evening:

Seven weeks ago tonight I returned from Europe to report on my meeting with [Soviet] Premier [Nikita] Khrushchev and the others. His grim warnings about the future of the world, his aide memoire on Berlin, his subsequent speeches and threats which he and his agents have launched, and the increase in the Soviet military budget that he has announced, have all prompted a series of decisions by the Administration and a series of consultations with the members of the NATO [North Atlantic Treaty Organiza-

John F. Kennedy, address to the American people, Washington, DC, July 25, 1961.

tion] organization. In Berlin, as you recall, he intends to bring to an end, through a stroke of the pen, *first* our legal rights to be in West Berlin—and *secondly* our ability to make good on our commitment to the two million free people of that city. That we cannot permit.

We are clear about what must be done—and we intend to do it. I want to talk frankly with you tonight about the first steps that we shall take. These actions will require sacrifice on the part of many of our citizens. More will be required in the future. They will require, from all of us, courage and perseverance in the years to come. But if we and our allies act out of strength and unity of purpose—with calm determination and steady nerves—using restraint in our words as well as our weapons—I am hopeful that both peace and freedom will be sustained.

The immediate threat to free men is in West Berlin. But that isolated outpost is not an isolated problem. The threat is worldwide. Our effort must be equally wide and strong, and not be obsessed by any single manufactured crisis. We face a challenge in Berlin, but there is also a challenge in Southeast Asia, where the borders are less guarded, the enemy harder to find, and the dangers of communism less apparent to those who have so little. We face a challenge in our own hemisphere, and indeed wherever else the freedom of human beings is at stake.

If we and our allies act out of strength and unity of purpose—with calm determination and steady nerves—. . . I am hopeful that both peace and freedom will be sustained.

Let me remind you that the fortunes of war and diplomacy left the free people of West Berlin, in 1945, 110 miles behind the Iron Curtain [the dividing line between free democracies and Soviet-controlled Communist nations]. . . .

West Berlin is 110 miles within the area which the Soviets now dominate—which is immediately controlled by the so-called East German regime.

We are there as a result of our victory over Nazi Germany—and our basic rights to be there, deriving from that victory, include both our presence in West Berlin and the enjoyment of access across East Germany. These rights have been repeatedly confirmed and recognized in special agreements with the Soviet Union. Berlin is not a part of East Germany, but a separate territory under the control of the allied powers. Thus our rights there are clear and deep-rooted. But in addition to those rights is our commitment to sustain—and defend, if need be—the opportunity for more than two million people to determine their own future and choose their own way of life.

A Test of Western Courage

Thus, our presence in West Berlin, and our access thereto, cannot be ended by any act of the Soviet government. The NATO shield was long ago extended to cover West Berlin—and we have given our word that an attack upon that city will be regarded as an attack upon us all.

For West Berlin—lying exposed 110 miles inside East Germany, surrounded by Soviet troops and close to Soviet supply lines, has many roles. It is more than a showcase of liberty, a symbol, an island of freedom in a Communist sea. It is even more than a link with the Free World, a beacon of hope behind the Iron Curtain, an escape hatch for refugees.

West Berlin is all of that. But above all it has now become—as never before—the great testing place of Western courage and will, a focal point where our solemn commitments stretching back over the years since 1945, and Soviet ambitions now meet in basic confrontation.

It would be a mistake for others to look upon Berlin, because of its location, as a tempting target. The United States is there; the United Kingdom and France are there; the pledge of NATO is there—and the people of Berlin are there. It is as secure, in that sense, as the rest of us—for we cannot separate its safety from our own.

I hear it said that West Berlin is militarily untenable. And so [in World War II] was Bastogne [Belgium]. And so, in fact, was Stalingrad [Russia]. Any dangerous spot is tenable if men—brave men—will make it so.

We do not want to fight—but we have fought before. And others in earlier times have made the same dangerous mistake of assuming that the West was too selfish and too soft and too divided to resist invasions of freedom in other lands. Those who threaten to unleash the forces of war on a dispute over West Berlin should recall the words of the ancient philosopher: "A man who causes fear cannot be free from fear."

We cannot and will not permit the Communists to drive us out of Berlin, either gradually or by force. For the fulfillment of our pledge to that city is essential to the morale and security of Western Germany, to the unity of Western Europe, and to the faith of the entire Free World. Soviet strategy has long been aimed, not merely at Berlin, but at dividing and neutralizing all of Europe, forcing us back on our own shores. We must meet our oft-stated pledge to the free peoples of West Berlin—and maintain our rights and their safety, even in the face of force—in order to maintain the confidence of other free peoples in our word and our resolve. The strength of the alliance on which our security depends is dependent in turn on our willingness to meet our commitments to them.

A Plan of Action

So long as the Communists insist that they are preparing to end by themselves unilaterally our rights in West Berlin and our commitments to its people, we must be prepared to defend those rights and those commitments. We will at all times be ready to talk, if talk will help. But we must also be ready to resist with force, if force is used upon us. Either alone would fail. Together, they can serve the cause of freedom and peace.

The new preparations that we shall make to defend the peace are part of the long-term build-up in our strength which has been underway since January. They are based on our needs to meet a world-wide threat, on a basis which stretches far beyond the present Berlin crisis. Our primary purpose is neither propaganda nor provocation—but preparation.

A first need is to hasten progress toward the military goals which the North Atlantic allies have set for themselves. In Europe today nothing less will suffice. We will put even greater resources into fulfilling those goals, and we look to our allies to do the same.

The supplementary defense build-ups that I asked from the Congress in March and May have already started moving us toward these and our other defense goals. They included an increase in the size of the Marine Corps, improved readiness of our reserves, expansion of our air and sea lift, and stepped-up procurement of needed weapons, ammunition, and other items. To insure a continuing invulnerable capacity to deter or destroy any aggressor, they provided for the strengthening of our missile power and for putting 50% of our B-52 and B-47 bombers on a ground alert which would send them on their way with 15 minutes' warning.

These measures must be speeded up, and still others must now be taken. We must have sea and air lift capable of moving our forces quickly and in large numbers to any part of the world.

But even more importantly, we need the capability of placing in any critical area at the appropriate time a force which, combined with those of our allies, is large enough to make clear our determination and our ability to defend our rights at all costs—and to meet all levels of aggressor pressure with whatever levels of force are required. We intend to have a wider choice than humiliation or all-out nuclear action.

While it is unwise at this time either to call up or send abroad excessive numbers of these troops before they are needed, let me make it clear that I intend to take, as time goes on, whatever steps are necessary to make certain that such forces can be deployed at the appropriate time without lessening our ability to meet our commitments elsewhere.

We cannot and will not permit the Communists to drive us out of Berlin, either gradually or by force.

Thus, in the days and months ahead, I shall not hesitate to ask the Congress for additional measures, or exercise any of the executive powers that I possess to meet this threat to peace. Everything essential to the security of freedom must be done; and if that should require more men, or more taxes, or more controls, or other new powers, I shall not hesitate to ask them. The measures proposed today will be constantly studied, and altered as necessary. But while we will not let panic shape our policy, neither will we permit timidity to direct our program.

Accordingly, I am now taking the following steps:
1. I am tomorrow requesting the Congress for the current fiscal year an additional $3,247,000,000 of appropriations for the Armed Forces.

2. To fill out our present Army Divisions, and to make more men available for prompt deployment, I am requesting an increase in the Army's total authorized strength from 875,000 to approximately 1 million men.

3. I am requesting an increase of 29,000 and 63,000 men respectively in the active duty strength of the Navy and the Air Force.

4. To fulfill these manpower needs, I am ordering that our draft calls be doubled and tripled in the coming months; I am asking the Congress for authority to order to active duty certain ready reserve units and individual reservists, and to extend tours of duty; and, under that authority, I am planning to order to active duty a number of air transport squadrons and Air National Guard tactical air squadrons, to give us the airlift capacity and protection that we need. Other reserve forces will be called up when needed.

5. Many ships and planes once headed for retirement are to be retained or reactivated, increasing our air power tactically and our sealift, airlift, and antisubmarine warfare capability. In addition, our strategic air power will be increased by delaying the deactivation of B-47 bombers.

6. Finally, some $1.8 billion—about half of the total sum—is needed for the procurement of non-nuclear weapons, ammunition and equipment.

The details on all these requests will be presented to the Congress tomorrow. Subsequent steps will be taken to suit subsequent needs. Comparable efforts for the common defense are being discussed with our NATO allies. For their commitment and interest are as precise as our own.

And let me add that I am well aware of the fact that many American families will bear the burden of these requests. Studies or careers will be interrupted; husbands and sons will be called away; incomes in some cases will be reduced. But these are burdens which must be borne if freedom is to be defended—Americans have willingly borne them before—and they will not flinch from the task now.

The Civil Defense

We have another sober responsibility. To recognize the possibilities of nuclear war in the missile age, without our citizens knowing what they should do and where they should go if bombs begin to fall, would be a failure of responsibility. In May, I pledged a new start on Civil Defense. Last week, I assigned, on the recommendation of the Civil Defense Director, basic responsibility for this program to the Secretary of Defense, to make certain it is administered and coordinated with our continental defense efforts at the highest civilian level. Tomorrow, I am requesting of the Congress new funds for the following immediate objectives: to identify and mark space in existing structures—public and private—that could be used for fall-out shelters in case of attack; to stock those shelters with food, water, first-aid kits and other minimum essentials for survival; to increase their capacity; to improve our air-raid warning and fallout detection systems, including a new household warning system which is now under development; and to take other measures that will be effective at an early date to save millions of lives if needed.

The source of world trouble and tension is Moscow, not Berlin. And if war begins, it will have begun in Moscow and not Berlin.

In the event of an attack, the lives of those families which are not hit in a nuclear blast and fire can still be saved—if they can be warned to take shelter and if that shelter is available. We owe that kind of insurance to our families—and to our country. In contrast to our friends in Europe, the need for this kind of protection is new to our shores. But the time to start is now. In the coming months, I hope to let every citizen know what steps he can take without delay to protect his family in case of attack. I know that you will want to do no less.

Budgetary Concerns

The addition of $207 million in Civil Defense appropriations brings our total new defense budget requests to $3.454 billion, and a total of $47.5 billion for the year. This is an increase in the defense budget of $6 billion since January, and has resulted in official estimates of a budget deficit of over $5 billion. The Secretary of the Treasury and other economic advisers assure me, however, that our economy has the capacity to bear this new request. . . .

I intend to submit to the Congress in January a budget for the next fiscal year which will be strictly in balance. Nevertheless, should an increase in taxes be needed—because of events in the next few months—to achieve that balance, or because of subsequent defense rises, those increased taxes will be requested in January.

Meanwhile, to help make certain that the current deficit is held to a safe level, we must keep down all expenditures not thoroughly justified in budget requests. The luxury of our current post-office deficit must be ended. Costs in military procurement will be closely scrutinized—and in this effort I welcome the cooperation of the Congress. The tax loopholes I have specified—on expense accounts, overseas income, dividends, interest, cooperatives and others—must be closed.

I realize that no public revenue measure is welcomed by everyone. But I am certain that every American wants to pay his fair share, and not leave the burden of defending freedom entirely to those who bear arms. For we have mortgaged our very future on this defense—and we cannot fail to meet our responsibilities.

A Commitment to Peace

But I must emphasize again that the choice is not merely between resistance and retreat, between atomic holocaust and surrender. Our peace-time military posture is traditionally defensive; but our diplomatic posture need not be. Our response to the Berlin crisis will not be merely military or negative. It will be more than merely standing firm. For we do not intend to leave it to others to choose and monopolize the forum and the framework of discussion. We do not intend to abandon our duty to mankind to seek a peaceful solution. As signers of the UN [United Nations] Charter, we shall always be prepared to discuss international problems with any and all nations that are willing to talk—and listen—with reason. If they have proposals—not demands—we shall hear them. If they seek genuine understanding—not concessions of our rights—we shall meet with them. We have previously indicated our readiness to remove any actual irritants in West Berlin, but the freedom of that city is not negotiable. We cannot negotiate with those who say "What's mine is mine and what's yours is negotiable." But we are willing to consider any arrangement or treaty in Germany consistent with the maintenance of peace and freedom, and with the legitimate security interests of all nations.

We recognize the Soviet Union's historical concern about their security in Central and Eastern Europe, after a series of ravaging invasions, and we believe arrangements can be worked out which will help to meet those concerns, and make it possible for both security and freedom to exist in this troubled area.

We seek peace—but we shall not surrender.

For it is not the freedom of West Berlin which is "abnormal" in Germany today, but the situation in that entire divided country. If anyone doubts the legality of our rights in Berlin, we are ready to have it submitted to international adjudication. If anyone doubts the extent to which our presence is desired by the people of West Berlin, compared to East German feelings about their regime, we are ready to have that question submitted to a free vote in Berlin and, if possible, among all the German people. And let us hear at that time from the two and one-half million refugees who have fled the Communist regime in East Germany—voting for Western-type freedom with their feet.

The world is not deceived by the Communist attempt to label Berlin as a hot-bed of war. There is peace in Berlin today. The source of world trouble and tension is Moscow, not Berlin. And if war begins, it will have begun in Moscow and not Berlin.

For the choice of peace or war is largely theirs, not ours. It is the Soviets who have stirred up this crisis. It is they who are trying to force a change. It is they who have opposed free elections. It is they who have rejected an all-German peace treaty, and the rulings of international law. And as Americans know from our history on our own old frontier, gun battles are caused by outlaws, and not by officers of the peace.

In short, while we are ready to defend our interests, we shall also be ready to search for peace—in quiet exploratory talks—in formal or informal meetings. We do not want military considerations to dominate the thinking of either East or West. And Mr. Khrushchev may find that his invitation to other nations to join in a meaningless treaty may lead to their inviting him to join in the community of peaceful men, in abandoning the use of force, and in respecting the sanctity of agreements.

The Challenge to Be Met

While all of these efforts go on, we must not be diverted from our total responsibilities, from other dangers, from other tasks. If new threats in Berlin or elsewhere should cause us to weaken our program of assistance to the developing nations who are also under heavy pressure from the same source, or to halt our efforts for realistic disarmament, or to disrupt or slow down our economy, or to neglect the education of our children, then those threats will surely be the most successful and least costly maneuver in Communist history. For we can afford all these efforts, and more— but we cannot afford not to meet this challenge.

And the challenge is not to us alone. It is a challenge to every nation which asserts its sovereignty under a system of liberty. It is a challenge to all those who want a world of free choice. It is a special challenge to the Atlantic Community [the United States and Western European nations]—the heartland of human freedom.

We in the West must move together in building military strength. We must consult one another more closely than ever before. We must together design our proposals for peace, and labor together as they are pressed at the conference table. And together we must share the burdens and the risks of this effort.

The Atlantic Community, as we know it, has been built in response to challenge: the challenge of European chaos in 1947, of the Berlin blockade in 1948, the challenge of Communist aggression in Korea in 1950. Now, standing strong and prosperous, after an unprecedented decade of progress, the Atlantic Community will not forget either its history or the principles which gave it meaning.

The solemn vow each of us gave to West Berlin in time of peace will not be broken in time of danger. If we do not meet our commitments to Berlin, where will we later stand? If we are not true to our word there, all that we have achieved in collective security, which relies on these words, will mean nothing. And if there is one path above all others to war, it is the path of weakness and disunity.

A Frontier of Peace

Today, the endangered frontier of freedom runs through divided Berlin. We want it to remain a frontier of peace. This is the hope of every citizen of the Atlantic Community; every citizen of Eastern Europe; and, I am confident, every citizen of the Soviet Union. For I cannot believe that the Russian people—who bravely suffered enormous losses in the Second World War would now wish to see the peace upset once more in Germany. The Soviet government alone can convert Berlin's frontier of peace into a pretext for war.

The steps I have indicated tonight are aimed at avoiding that war. To sum it all up: we seek peace—but we shall not surrender. That is the central meaning of this crisis, and the meaning of your government's policy.

With your help, and the help of other free men, this crisis can be surmounted. Freedom can prevail—and peace can endure.

I would like to close with a personal word. When I ran for the Presidency of the United States, I knew that this country faced serious challenges, but I could not realize—nor could any man realize who does not bear the burdens of this office—how heavy and constant would be those burdens.

Three times in my life-time our country and Europe have been involved in major wars. In each case serious misjudgments were made on both sides of the intentions of others, which brought about great devastation.

Now, in the thermonuclear age, any misjudgment on either side about the intentions of the other could rain more devastation in several hours than has been wrought in all the wars of human history.

Therefore I, as President and Commander-in-Chief, and all of us as Americans, are moving through serious days. I shall bear this responsibility under our Constitution for the next three and one-half years, but I am sure that we all, regardless of our occupations, will do our very best for our country, and for our cause. For all of us want to see our children grow up in a country at peace, and in a world where freedom endures.

I know that sometimes we get impatient, we wish for some immediate action that would end our perils. But I must tell you that there is no quick and easy solution. The Communists control over a billion people, and they recognize that if we should falter, their success would be imminent.

We must look to long days ahead, which if we are courageous and persevering can bring us what we all desire.

In these days and weeks I ask for your help, and your advice. I ask for your suggestions, when you think we could do better.

All of us, I know, love our country, and we shall all do our best to serve it.

In meeting my responsibilities in these coming months as President, I need your good will, and your support—and above all, your prayers.

Thank you, and good night.

4

The East Will Not Withdraw from Berlin

Nikita S. Khrushchev

On August 3–5, 1961, in response to President Kennedy's speech on July 25, the Soviet premier Nikita S. Khrushchev met with officials from six other Communist-ruled countries from Eastern Europe to discuss the possibility of war with the West. The following selection contains excerpts from his speech given during the second session on August 4.

Premier Khrushchev urges Eastern leaders to press for a peace treaty with the West. He discusses his meeting in July with an envoy of the United States in which he had stated that he would not declare war but that the Soviets would not withdraw from one either. However, Premier Khrushchev believes that war is unlikely because of the great destruction possible from atomic weapons. Lastly, he makes a case for supporting East Germany economically, saying that without this support, it will crumble and the Western allies will move in. (Bracketed information was provided for greater understanding by the editors of the CNN Cold War website.)

O ur delegation agrees completely with what Comrade [Walter] Ulbricht [of East Germany] has reported . . . We must wring this peace treaty . . . They [the Western powers] had hauled Germany into the Western bloc, and Germany became split into two parts. The peace treaty will give legitimacy to this split . . . it will weaken the West and,

Nikita S. Khrushchev, "The Conference of First Secretaries of Central Committees of Communist and Workers Parties of Socialist Countries for the Exchange of Views on the Questions Related to Preparation and Conclusion of German Peace Treaty, 3–5 August 1961. (Khrushchev's Secret Speech on the Berlin Crisis, August 1961)," www.turnerlearning.com, August 4, 1961. Copyright © 1961 by the Cold War International History Project. Reproduced by permission.

49

of course, the West will not agree with it. Their eviction from West Berlin will mean closing of the channels for their subversive activities against us. . . .

I believe there are people in our countries who might argue: was it worth a cost to push this issue and let the heat and international tension rise . . . We have to explain to them that we have to wring this peace treaty, there is no other way . . . Every action produces counteraction, hence they resist fiercely . . . [There was always an understanding, Khrushchev continued, that the West] would intimidate us, call out all spirits against us to test our courage, our acumen and our will.

We have to wring this peace treaty, there is no other way.

As for me and my colleagues in the state and party leadership, we think that the adversary proved to be less staunch than we had estimated . . . We expected there would be more blustering and . . . so far the worst spurt of intimidation was in the Kennedy speech [on 25 July 1961] . . . Kennedy spoke [to frighten us] and then got scared himself . . . Immediately after Kennedy delivered his speech I spoke with [U.S. envoy John J. McCloy]. We had a long conversation, talking about disarmament instead of talking, as we needed to, about Germany and conclusion of a peace treaty on West Berlin. So I suggested: come to my place [Black Sea resort in Pitsunda] tomorrow and we will continue our conversation.

Kennedy Has Declared War

On the first day [in Pitsunda] before talking we followed a Roman rite by taking a swim in a pool. We got our picture taken, embraced together . . . I have no idea whom he is going to show this picture to, but I don't care to appear on one picture with a Wall Street representative in the Soviet pool. I said [to McCloy]: 'I don't understand what sort of disarmament we can talk about, when Kennedy in his speech declared war on us and set down his conditions. What can I say? Please tell your president that we accept his ultimatum and his terms and will respond in kind.'

He then said . . . [that] Kennedy did not mean it, he meant to negotiate. I responded: 'Mr. McCloy, but you said you did not read Kennedy's speech?' He faltered, for clearly he knew about the content of the speech . . . .'You want to frighten us,' I went on [to McCloy]. 'You convinced yourself, that Khrushchev will never go to war . . . so you scare us [expecting] us to retreat. True, we will not declare war, but we will not withdraw either, if you push it on us. We will respond to your war in kind.'

I told him to let Kennedy know . . . that if he starts a war then he would probably become the last president of the United States of America. I know he reported it accurately. In America they are showing off vehemently, but yet people close to Kennedy are beginning to pour cold water like a fire-brigade.

We already passed that age, we wear long trousers, not short ones.

There Will Be No War

I told [Amintore] Fanfani [the prime minister of Italy] yesterday: '. . . I don't believe, though, there will be war. What am I counting on? I believe in your [Western leaders'] common sense. Do you know who will argue most against war? [Konrad] Adenauer [chancellor of the West German Republic]. [Because, if the war starts] there will not be a single stone left in place in Germany . . .'

[War between the USSR and the United States, Khrushchev allegedly told Fanfani, is] hardly possible, because it would be a duel of ballistic intercontinental missiles. We are strong on that . . . America would be at a disadvantage to start a war with this weapon . . . They know it and admit it . . . America can unleash a war from its military bases they have on [Italian] territory. Consequently we consider you as our hostages.

If [Kennedy] starts a war then he would probably become the last president of the United States of America.

[British Prime Minister Harold Macmillan visited Moscow in 1959 and told Khrushchev that war was impossible. Khrushchev presumes that Western leaders continue to act on that conviction.] Macmillan could not have lost his mind since then. He considered war impossible then and, suddenly, now he changes his mind? No, no. The outcome of modern war will be decided by atomic weapons. Does it make sense if there is one more division or less? If the entire French army cannot cope with the Algerians, armed with knives, then how do they expect to scare us with a division? It is ludicrous, not frightening. [De Gaulle admitted to our Ambassador a couple of weeks ago, Khrushchev says, that he did not want the reunification of Germany.] He pays lip service to it [reunification] because it is in Adenauer's interests. Nobody wants reunification of Germany—neither France, nor England, nor Italy, nor America.

Anything is possible in the United States. War is also possible. They can unleash it.

[If Western powers refuse to sign a treaty with the GDR [East Germany], then, as Khrushchev said to McCloy:] You will have no access [to West Berlin]. If you fly and violate [the aerial space over the GDR], we will down your planes, you must know it.

Why we were so blunt? Comrades, we have to demonstrate to them our will and decisiveness . . . .

Hence anything is possible in the United States. War is also possible. They can unleash it. There are more stable situations in England, France, Italy, Germany. I would even say that, when our 'friend' [John Foster] Dulles [U.S. secretary of state] was alive, they had more stability [in the United States]. I told McCloy about it.

[Dulles was the enemy who] resolved to bring us down to submission, but he was afraid of war. He would reach the brink, as he put it himself, but he would never leap over the brink, and [nevertheless] retained his credibility.

On our side, we have already mapped out some measures. And we are considering more in the future, but short of provocations. I told McCloy, that if they deploy one division in Germany, we will respond with two divisions, if they declare mobilization, we will do the same. If they mobilize such and such numbers, we will put out 150–200 divisions, as many as necessary. We are considering now . . . to deploy tanks defensively along the entire border [between East and West Germany]. In short, we have to seal every weak spot they might look for.

Supporting East Germany
[Khrushchev doubted that Western powers would risk to force their way to West Berlin, because it would surely mean war. But he said that chances of economic blockade of the GDR and, perhaps, of the entire Eastern bloc were "fifty-fifty." That led him to comment ruefully on the dependence of socialist economies on Western trade and loans:] We have to help the GDR out . . . Everybody is guilty, and the GDR too. We let down our guards somewhat. Sixteen years passed and we did not alleviate pressures on the GDR. . . .

[He conceded that the GDR, if not helped, will collapse.] What will it mean, if the GDR is liquidated? It will mean that the Bundeswehr [German defense forces] will move to the Polish border, . . . to the borders with Czechoslovakia, . . . closer to our Soviet border. [He then addressed another point of criticism, why it was necessary to help the GDR to raise its living standard, already the highest among the countries in the Eastern bloc:] If we level it [the GDR's living standard] down to our own, consequently, the government and the party of the GDR will fall down tumbling, consequently Adenauer will step in . . . Even if the GDR remains closed, one cannot rely on that and [let living standards decline].

I wish we could lick the imperialism! You can imagine what satisfaction we'll get when we sign the peace treaty. Of course we're running a risk. But it is indispensable. Lenin took such a risk, when he said in 1917 that there was such a party that could seize power. Everybody just smirked and snorted then . . . World public opinion now is on our side not only in the neutral countries, but in America and in England.

Summing up, our Central Committee and government believe, that now preparations are proceeding better, but there will be a thaw, and, more importantly, a cooling down . . . We have to work out our tactics now and perhaps it is already the right time.

Chapter 2

The Construction of the Berlin Wall

1

The Wall Was a Result of Tensions Between the Soviet Union and East Germany

Hope M. Harrison

Through archival research and personal interviews with East German officials, Hope M. Harrison catalogs a troubled relationship between the Soviet Union and East Germany from the latter's foundation in 1945 through the construction of the Berlin Wall in 1961. She finds that Walter Ulbricht, leader of the German Democratic Republic (East Germany), played upon the desires of Soviet leader Nikita Khrushchev to make East Germany a showplace for the success of Communist policies.

Ulbricht, by making unpopular and unilateral economic policy decisions, instigated a mass emigration from East Germany. This exodus forced the Soviets to allow him to build a wall between East and West Berlin, giving Ulbricht tighter, dictatorial control over the East German state. Harrison is assistant professor in the department of government and law at Lafayette College.

There was more conflict between the Soviet and East German leaderships in the early cold war period than is generally known. East German hard-liners used the weakness of their regime's hold on power as leverage in

Hope M. Harrison, "Soviet–East German Relations After World War II," *Problems of Post-Communism*, vol. 42, September/October 1995, p. 9. Copyright © 1995 by M.E. Sharpe, Inc. Reproduced by permission.

their bargaining with the Soviet Union.

World War II left a bitter legacy for relations between the peoples of Germany and the Soviet Union. Fifty years later, former Soviet citizens have not forgotten that a mutual nonaggression pact failed to stop a brutal German invasion of the Soviet Union, and Germans still recall the savagery of the Red Army's drive to Berlin. The heavy-handed Soviet treatment of its German occupation zone and later the East German state only exacerbated the tensions in their relations, especially since many Germans felt culturally superior to the Slavs. The first fifteen years after the end of World War II, however, witnessed a drastic reversal in Soviet treatment of East Germany from exploitation to building up the German Democratic Republic (GDR) as the "showcase of socialism." This article explores the process of this change and the increasingly complex relations between the Soviet Union and East Germany leading up to the construction of the Berlin Wall in 1961. Soviet and East German archives have now revealed that there was more East German influence over events in East Germany and Berlin and over Soviet policy in these areas than has been previously acknowledged.

Revenge and Rebuild

As Norman Naimark details in his new book, *The Soviet Occupation of Germany*, Moscow's immediate postwar policies in the Soviet occupation zone were dominated by a desire for revenge and a need to rebuild the ravaged Soviet economy. German women were raped by Soviet soldiers, whole German factories were dismantled and transported by train to the Soviet Union, and food needed by desperate German citizens was taken to feed desperate Soviet citizens. One-quarter of the industrial equipment in the eastern zone of Germany was appropriated by the Soviet forces, making the eastern zone particularly vulnerable since Germany's main industrial areas were in the western zones.

Not only did the Soviet leaders want to punish the Germans by taking everything they could to help rebuild their own country; they also wanted to prevent Germany from regaining the capacity to invade their territory for a third time in the twentieth century. While the Soviet Union continued its plunder, the United States, Great Britain, and France fostered recovery in their zones of Germany and began seeing the western Germans as potential allies against communism. Soviet and Western policy regarding Germany, therefore, came increasingly into conflict and contributed to the onset of the cold war, the division of Germany, and persistent East German economic difficulties. Indeed, as late as 1961, East German leader Walter Ulbricht was still reminding Soviet leader Nikita S. Khrushchev that if East Germany had received the kind of aid that West Germany received from the United States in the first postwar decade, the East German economy would not have been so weak. This became an important line of argument, although more often implied than directly stated, as the East Germans attempted to procure more and more Soviet aid.

Division Becomes Permanent

For various reasons, Soviet policy toward East Germany shifted from massive extractions of goods in the late 1940s and early 1950s to massive infusions of goods, money, and know-how into East Germany in the mid-to late 1950s and afterward. These reasons include Western policy toward West Germany, East German bargaining tactics with the Soviet Union, and Khrushchev's own views of the importance of a stable East Germany. Although the four victorious allies of Word War II occupied and divided Germany and Berlin into zones at the end of the war, they originally did not intend or expect that either occupation or division would be permanent. [Joseph] Stalin [the Soviet leader until 1953], in particular, seems to have held on to the notion of a united Germany longer than his Western counterparts did. He hoped for a united, neutral Germany that would be friendlier to the Soviet Union and communism than to the West and capitalism. Only in the face of persistent Western policies to institute democracy and capitalism in the Western zones and then to form and arm a West German state did Stalin become resigned to forming and developing an East German state. Stalin's attempt to prevent the formation and stabilization of a West German state by blockading Berlin from 1948 to 1949, and the successful Western airlift to the western zones of Berlin, were crucial steps in this process.

After the Berlin blockade, Stalin made one other notable attempt to change the situation in Germany to his advantage. He sent a note to the Western powers on March 10, 1952, proposing the formation of a united, neutral Germany with its own defensive military forces. Although the debate about the sincerity of Stalin's intentions in this note rages on, recent archival evidence described by Gerhard Wettig and Ruud van Dijk indicates that Stalin sent the note only after being assured by his Foreign Ministry advisers that the West would not accept his proposals. Thus, the note was just the best-known step in the propaganda battle between East and West. Each side tried to prove to the German people that it was more concerned with restoring unity to Germany than the other side and thus deserved the allegiance of the German people. The note was also an unsuccessful attempt to stop the rearmament of West Germany and its integration into a Western military alliance.

Moscow's immediate postwar policies in the Soviet occupation zone were dominated by a desire for revenge and a need to rebuild the ravaged Soviet economy.

Meanwhile, the core of communist German leaders in the Soviet zone of Germany were eager to create their own state and institute socialism. During World War II, Walter Ulbricht, the head of the ruling East German Socialist Unity Party (SED), and other prominent East German communists had sought protection in the Soviet Union from the Nazi dictatorship in Germany. In the Soviet Union, they were organized as the National Committee for Free Germany and trained in the methods of Soviet rule so that after the war they could return to Germany, attempt to take power in all of Germany, and ally Germany with the Soviet Union. Ulbricht, Wilhelm Pieck, Otto Grotewohl, and other German leaders were strongly motivated to establish a Soviet-backed German regime, as they would have lost their leadership positions, perhaps their lives, should their plans for Germany not succeed. This East German raison d'etre [justification for existence] led to a situation in which even when Stalin and his successors, including Mikhail Gorbachev, were wavering as to just what kind of state they desired in East Germany, the East German leaders pushed strongly for a rigid socialist state, since this was the only way they could justify having their own state separate from that of West Germany.

The Soviet leadership had a broader range of goals in mind for Germany than the East German leadership did, and this led to conflicts between the two sets of leaders, beginning in the immediate postwar period and extending until the collapse of East Germany in 1989 and 1990. Whenever Moscow felt the need for more cordial relations with the West—and with West Germany specifically—East Germany would raise objections or obstacles. Frequently, the East German regime would tighten its control within East Germany and over relations between East and West Germans, knowing that the West would always think the Soviet leaders were behind this clamping down and thus feel more hostile toward Moscow.

Soviet Reforms Rejected

One of the earliest, most significant examples of the conflict between the Soviet Union and East Germany over the nature of the East German regime—and East German relations with West Germany—occurred just after Stalin's death in the spring of 1953. Stalin's successors, Nikita Khrushchev, Georgii Malenkov, and Lavrenty Beria, sought to chart a new course in Soviet foreign policy and reduce tensions in relations with the West, so that they could focus on improving domestic conditions in the Soviet Union. Accordingly, the new Soviet leaders told the East German regime to slacken the pace of their "Construction of Socialism" program. They felt that the East German policies of rapid industrialization and collectivization, originally implemented with Soviet approval, had been too harsh on the East German people as indicated by the increasing numbers of people fleeing East Germany for the West.

Whenever Moscow felt the need for more cordial relations with the West—and with West Germany specifically—East Germany would raise objections or obstacles.

As is documented in archives in Berlin and Moscow, on June 2, 1953, the Soviet Union presented the East German leadership with a resolution for a "New Course" in policy, detailing "measures for the recovery of the political situation in the German Democratic Republic." The New Course sought to reduce the refugee exodus by improving the East German standard of living, toning down ideological campaigns, relieving pressure on the churches, relaxing the tempo of the development of heavy industry and collectivization, developing better relations with West Germany (especially the Social Democratic Party), and making more concerted and public efforts to bring about German reunification and the conclusion of a German peace treaty (which had still not been concluded because of differences among the victors). To help the East Germans institute more liberal, friendly policies, the Soviet leaders promised to alleviate their reparations payments and to supply more raw materials and food.

The spring of 1953 marked the beginning of Soviet and later West German efforts (motivated by different factors) to persuade the East German leadership to institute more liberal policies to satisfy the East German population, coupled with the provision of Soviet and later West German economic support to promote the institution of these more liberal policies. However, archival research in Berlin and Moscow reveals that the East Germans consistently used Soviet and then West German economic aid, for what Timothy Garton Ash describes as "reform substitution" instead of "reform promotion." The East German leadership used the aid to try to buy off the population by giving them more consumer goods instead of creating more democratic institutions and processes in East Germany. The East Germans used this tactic from 1953 until 1989, when it clearly failed.

East Germans Revolt

In 1953, Ulbricht did not institute all the changes the Soviet Union specified in the New Course and certainly not to the degree intended. In addition to the fact that Ulbricht needed to distinguish East Germany clearly from West Germany, his dictatorial proclivities made him wary of relinquishing any power. Since he was eager to expand the industrial production of East Germany as soon as possible, Ulbricht did not reduce the production quotas he had raised by 10 percent earlier in the spring. The partial liberalization East Germans received from the New Course, combined with the increased work norms, led to mass worker demonstrations in Berlin on June 16. By June 17, the rally turned into a full-fledged uprising in Berlin and 250 other towns in East Germany. The workers were joined by other citizens, and their demands evolved from reducing the work quotas to having more political freedoms and ousting the East German leadership.

While the panicky East German leadership was kept safe at Soviet headquarters at Karlshorst near Berlin, Soviet tanks suppressed the uprising. Over forty people were killed, and more than 4,000 people were arrested. By June 20, the Soviet forces and the East German regime were again in control of the country. . . .

Soviets Begin Support

The uprising made it clear, as Soviet Prime Minister Malenkov had noted, that "without the presence of Soviet troops, the existing regime in the GDR was not durable." Thus, if the new Soviet leadership was going to guarantee the success of the East German regime, it was clearly going to have to do a lot more investing in East Germany and a lot less looting of it. Accordingly, on June 24, 1953, the Soviet leaders told the East Germans that (at last) they would satisfy their requests for significant increases in supplies of foodstuffs and cotton and also that they would augment their supply and training of the East German People's Police.

Another factor in the new Soviet leadership's change of policy toward East Germany was the ouster and execution of the Soviet secret police chief, Lavrenty Beria. Among the charges leveled against Beria was that in the discussions within the Soviet leadership regarding the New Course in East Germany, Beria had proposed halting the Construction of Socialism program in East Germany, instead of just slowing it down. He allegedly felt that it was not worth the Soviet investments to make the program successful and that Soviet relations with the West would be greatly improved if the Soviet Union gave up East Germany and allowed it to be reunited with West Germany. Although the main reasons for Beria's ouster and execution had far more to do with his attempt to succeed Stalin, the fact that this alleged traitor to the Soviet cause had proposed giving up East Germany meant that any such talk was thereafter banished from the Soviet leadership.

The Soviet commitment to Ulbricht himself as the East

German leader also increased at this time. There were allegations that Beria had been allied with Ulbricht's main liberal rivals, Rudolf Herrnstadt (editor-in-chief of the main party newspaper, Neues Deutschland, and a Politburo member) and Wilhelm Zaisser (secret police chief and a Politburo member). Thus, as soon as Ulbricht learned (on July 7, 1953) of Beria's ouster, he sacked Herrnstadt and Zaisser, probably with Soviet approval. Although some Soviet leaders had supported Herrnstadt and Zaisser in May and June, believing they might institute a more stable and successful regime in East Germany than Ulbricht had done, Beria's alleged ties with them, and the Kremlin's reluctance to adopt any policy similar to Beria's, led the remaining Soviet leaders to support Ulbricht's continued leadership.

The clearest indications of what would remain Khrushchev's policy of profound commitment to communism in East Germany and Ulbricht as the East German ruler were the policies announced at the first Soviet–East German summit in Moscow in August 1953. The Soviet Union upgraded its official relations with East Germany, ended all reparations taken from East Germany by the Soviet Union and Poland as of January 1, 1954, canceled all East German debt to the Soviet Union, and increased significantly Soviet monetary aid, food, and consumer goods, and Soviet public diplomatic support for East Germany. Ulbricht deduced that when he and his regime were weak, the Soviet Union would come to his aid. He would come to count on this as the 1950s went on and especially with the onset of the Berlin crisis in 1958. . . . Moreover, his weakness could translate into bargaining strength with the Soviet Union.

The GDR's Symbolic Value

The Soviet commitment to promote the development of East German socialism grew partly from the GDR's symbolic value. Khrushchev, who by 1955 had won the post-Stalin succession struggle, believed deeply in the importance of the triumph of communism over capitalism in Germany, the homeland of Karl Marx and the place where the competing political systems came into the closest contact. Given the existence of nuclear weapons and the great risks involved in their use, Khrushchev believed that the main arenas for the competition between socialism and capitalism were economic and ideological. He wanted to win this competition in the place where it would be most visible to the West: East Germany, the westernmost member of the Soviet bloc. This necessitated much Soviet economic aid, since, as Khrushchev noted in his memoirs, "ideological issues are decided by the stomach, that is, by seeing who can provide the most for the people's daily needs. . . . The attraction of one or the other system is literally decided by the shop windows, by the price of goods, and by wages." Khrushchev also recognized that if communism collapsed in East Germany and it was absorbed into West Germany, the Western military alliance would move eastward, closer to Eastern Europe and the Soviet Union, an eventuality he wished to avoid.

Ulbricht deduced that when he and his regime were weak, the Soviet Union would come to his aid. He would come to count on this.

At the height of the Berlin crisis in June 1961, Prime Minister Anastas Mikoyan expressed to top East German economic officials the special importance of the GDR to the Soviet Union: "If socialism does not win in the GDR, if communism does not prove itself as superior and vital there, then we have not won. The issue is this fundamental to us. Therefore, we cannot proceed in such a way with any other country. And this is also the reason that the GDR occupies first place in negotiations or in credits." This knowledge of Khrushchev's profound commitment to communism's success in East Germany ultimately gave Ulbricht bargaining power, since he could claim that this would occur only if Khrushchev gave him what he requested, from economic aid and political control within East Germany to control over the borders between East and West Berlin.

As Soviet economic and diplomatic support for East Germany grew after 1953, Moscow remained dissatisfied with East German efforts to stem the refugee exodus. In 1955, a high-level Soviet Foreign Ministry official declared that the East German regime was still not taking the refugee problem seriously enough and was not instituting sufficiently "humane" policies to deal with the grievances of the population. In other words, the concerns that had led the Soviet leadership to demand the institution of the New

Course in East Germany in 1953 to halt the refugee exodus had still not been satisfied in 1955. This is probably the primary reason the Soviet Union supported a new challenger to Ulbricht after Khrushchev's "secret speech" in February 1956, calling for de-Stalinization and liberalization policies within the Soviet Union and East Europe. East German Politburo member Karl Schirdewan took Khrushchev's calls at the Twentieth Party Congress for "peaceful coexistence," "separate paths to socialism," and de-Stalinization seriously. He sought to improve East German living conditions, to institute more liberal economic and political practices at all levels of society, and to develop more friendly relations with West Germany. Archival documents in Moscow and Berlin reveal just how close the Soviet officials came to supporting Schirdewan's ouster of Ulbricht, since Schirdewan was clearly more willing to make the changes in East German policy the Soviet leaders thought necessary to stem the refugee exodus. However, just as with Herrnstadt and Zaisser in 1953, a combination of events in Eastern Europe (uprisings in Poland and Hungary in 1956) and within the Soviet Union (the unsuccessful yet powerful hard-line challenge to Khrushchev's leadership by the "anti-party group" in 1957) led the Soviet leadership to favor the continuity of Ulbricht over the unknown implicit in a new East German leadership.

Increased Soviet Commitment

Once Khrushchev had weathered the challenges in Eastern Europe and Moscow, he increased the Soviet commitment to the socialist triumph of East Germany. At the Fifth Congress of the SED in July 1958, Khrushchev supported Ulbricht's plan for East German per capita consumption to surpass that of West Germany in 1961. The only hope of meeting this target was massive Soviet aid. Khrushchev launched the Berlin crisis in November 1958 in part as a way to couple economic aid with political efforts to achieve stability in the GDR. On November 27, 1958, Khrushchev sent notes to the Western powers threatening that if a German peace treaty was not signed and a demilitarized "free city" of West Berlin was not created within six months, he would sign a separate peace treaty with East Germany, turning over to the East Germans control of the access routes across 110 miles of East German territory between West

Germany and West Berlin. The clear implication was that Ulbricht would institute a much more restrictive policy regarding access between West Berlin and West Germany, thus leading to conditions similar to those of the Soviet blockade of Berlin during 1948–49. From the Western standpoint, it was illegal for Khrushchev to cut off Western access to Berlin, since this had been guaranteed by agreements with the Soviet Union. Similarly, it was illegal for him unilaterally to transfer control over those access routes to the East Germans.

Since the movement of refugees from East to West was the clearest indication that communism was not triumphant in Germany, Khrushchev was eager to take steps to resolve this problem.

Khrushchev clearly hoped to gain Western recognition of the legitimacy of the East German regime, which he thought would help stabilize the situation in East Germany and stem the refugee exodus. He also assumed that making West Berlin into a "free city" would stop it from being a capitalist magnet for East German citizens and a base for Western espionage and anticommunist propaganda. East Germans would then be much less likely to want to leave the country. At the time Khrushchev issued his ultimatum, over 90 percent of East German refugees were escaping via West Berlin and usually going on to West Germany, so Khrushchev was intent on making it much more difficult for East Germans to get to West Berlin and points west.

The Refugee Problem

Since the movement of refugees from East to West was the clearest indication that communism was not triumphant in Germany, Khrushchev was eager to take steps to resolve this problem. In 1957 and throughout the Berlin crisis, there were at least monthly Soviet–East German meetings on the refugee problem with consistently urgent Soviet appeals (in vain) to the East German regime to deal with the population in a less bureaucratic and heartless way. The Soviet Union was especially concerned that the harsh East German policies were alienating the intelligentsia and causing rising numbers of them to emigrate. Thus, while Khrushchev was doing what he could internationally to try to change the structure of the situation facing the East German regime, he urged the East German leadership "not to act unilaterally" and "not to take any measures that could exacerbate the situation," that is, increase the refugee exodus or challenge Western access to Berlin.

Ulbricht, however, remained uninterested in loosening his hold on power in East Germany, which he feared would ultimately lead to his downfall. He also grew increasingly frustrated as two years had passed since Khrushchev's ultimatum, yet the Soviet leader still had not acted on his threats. There had been various conferences of the foreign ministers of the Soviet Union, the United States, Great Britain, and France, and Khrushchev had met with President Dwight Eisenhower at Camp David, but still the West had not given in to Khrushchev's demands, nor had Khrushchev carried out his threats. Meanwhile, the refugee exodus increased, spurred on both by Khrushchev's rhetoric and by Ulbricht's stepped-up agricultural collectivization. Both before and during the crisis, Ulbricht, other East German officials, and sympathetic Soviet officials frequently referred to the difficulties for East Germany due to the "open borders" or "lack of a closed border" in Berlin. Ulbricht wanted to close the border.

Ulbricht Takes Charge

In September 1960, Ulbricht finally took matters into his own hands. Since the West did not recognize the East German state, the Four Powers had agreed that Western officials entering East Germany had only to show their documents to Soviet—not East German border officials. On September 21, 1960, the East German regime announced that Western diplomats had to obtain permission from the East German Foreign Ministry to enter the country. Documents from East German archives indicate that this action was taken without prior consultation with, or approval from, the Soviet Union. Indeed, Soviet officials were "astounded" and infuriated by the unilateral East German action, fearing it might become more difficult for Soviet diplomats to travel to West Germany and West Berlin and might harm their campaign to get the West to sign a German peace treaty and create a free city in West Berlin. Although Soviet leaders were clearly critical of this East German behavior in private, in public they backed up the East German "sovereign right" to take these measures.

Khrushchev undoubtedly came to see the wall not only as a way to save the GDR . . . but also as a way to wall in Ulbricht in East Berlin.

Worried by East Germany's unilateral action, Khrushchev met with Ulbricht in Moscow in November. At this meeting, Khrushchev insisted that Ulbricht refrain from any more unilateral actions until Khrushchev had met the new American president, John F. Kennedy. In the meantime, Khrushchev virtually agreed to take over the East German economy in an effort to stem the refugee exodus. Khrushchev declared: "East German needs are our needs," and vowed that he would never treat East Germany the way Beria had wanted to in 1953. Khrushchev also promised Ulbricht that if he did not reach an agreement with the Western powers on a German peace treaty in 1961, he would sign a separate peace treaty with East Germany by the end of the year.

Ulbricht remained suspicious. More than two years had passed without Khrushchev fulfilling his promises to Ulbricht and his threats to the West. In a move that must have been calculated to put pressure on Khrushchev, Ulbricht dispatched a high-level delegation to Beijing in January 1961, as the widening schism between the Soviet Union and China reached its climax. When the delegation made a stopover in Moscow on the way to China, Soviet officials were again caught by surprise by East German actions. Contrary to normal Soviet bloc practice, the Kremlin had received no advance notice of, this East German trip to what was becoming a key enemy of the Soviet Union, to say nothing of having their approval solicited. Both East Germany and China claimed territory occupied by "imperialists"—West Berlin and Taiwan—and thought that the Soviet Union was not doing enough to help them recapture their lands. The East German trip was a shrewd attempt by Ulbricht to increase his maneuvering room within the Soviet bloc.

Ulbricht did persuade Khrushchev to convene a Warsaw Pact meeting in Moscow at the end of March 1961 to discuss Ulbricht's desire to close the border to West Berlin. At this meeting, the Soviet and other delegations agreed to go forward with Ulbricht's plan if Khrushchev could not come to an agreement with Kennedy and other Western leaders on a peace treaty and the free city of West Berlin. Again, Ulbricht was ordered not to take any unilateral actions in the meantime, and again high-level Soviet diplomats in Berlin informed Moscow afterward that the East Germans wanted "to close 'the door to the West' now" and that they were "exercising impatience and a somewhat unilateral approach to this problem."

Ulbricht Forces the Issue

Ulbricht also pushed the pace after Khrushchev and Kennedy failed to come to an agreement at the Vienna summit in early June 1961 at which Khrushchev gave Kennedy another ultimatum. Two weeks after the summit, during a news conference in East Berlin, Ulbricht asserted that a separate Soviet peace treaty with the GDR would give GDR authorities control over the access routes to Berlin. He also insisted, out of the blue, that "nobody has the intention of building a wall." These comments may have been made knowing that they would result in an increased refugee exodus, which they did, and that this would then finally force Khrushchev to "close the door to the West." More than 100,000 refugees fled the GDR in the first half of 1961, including 20,000 in June. In July 1,000 refugees left every day, with a total of 30,000 for the month.

According to Yuli Kvitsinsky, who was then a Soviet diplomat in Berlin, in late June or early July, Ulbricht invited him and Soviet ambassador Mikhail Pervukhin to his country house and asked Pervukhin to inform Khrushchev that "if the present situation of open borders remains, collapse is inevitable." Ulbricht "refused all responsibility for what would then happen" and "could not guarantee that he could keep the situation under control this time." After consulting with Khrushchev, Pervukhin told Ulbricht that Khrushchev had agreed to close the border, although Ulbricht was instructed that he must begin with barbed wire to test the Western reaction and only make the border closure more permanent if there was no strong Western reaction. East German secret police documents reveal that the code name for the plan to close the border was "Rose." Again Ulbricht found that the weakness of his regime, manifested in the refugee crisis, strengthened his bargaining power with Khrushchev. Finally, Khrushchev gave in to Ulbricht's persistent demand to close the border. The combination of Ulbricht's emphasis on the need to close the border to West Berlin in meetings and correspondence with Khrushchev, his faits accomplis [an irreversible decision] on the border, and his continuing harsh domestic policies, combined with Western intransigence, eventually convinced Khrushchev to erect the wall. By the summer of 1961, Krushchev undoubtedly came to see the wall not only as a way to save the GDR by stemming the refugee exodus and shoring up the economy but also as a way to wall in Ulbricht in East Berlin so that he could not make any more unilateral moves that could risk conflict with the West. Ulbricht's consistent hard-line course from 1953 through 1961 ultimately had narrowed Soviet policy options. Instead of building a wall, which Khrushchev later said made clear that East Germany was hardly the paradise claimed, he would have preferred a more successful East German economy recognized by the West. Ulbricht's harsh policies made all of this difficult to achieve.

2

Western Response to the Construction of the Berlin Wall Was Appropriate

Eric Morris

In this selection, Eric Morris traces the build up of tensions between the Soviet Union and Western powers that culminated in the Berlin crisis and the building of the Berlin Wall. Morris believes the construction of the wall to be a logical response to the crisis. While Western inaction was criticized because the East German move was a breach of earlier agreements, Morris asserts that even a limited response from the West might have elicited a strong overreaction from the Soviets, possibly leading to nuclear war.

The years which saw the great debate over the European Defence Community and the emergence of the Federal Republic of West Germany as a nation with full sovereignty had been relatively quiet for West Berlin. While Europe concerned itself with the broader issues of continental security, the municipal authorities could proceed with their own programme for social and economic reconstruction in what had temporarily become a backwater of international politics. However, after 1955 events took a different course: by his actions in the ensuing years, [premier of the Soviet Union Nikita S.] Khrushchev ensured that Berlin would re-

Eric Morris, *Blockade: Berlin and the Cold War*. London: Hamish Hamilton, 1973.

70

main central to all negotiations between the super-powers concerning Europe, and that no agreements over the status of the city could henceforth be reached without reference to broader European issues. For Khrushchev, West Berlin symbolized the threat to the Soviet empire in Eastern Europe. Russia had annexed part of German territory, had handed another part over to Poland, and now held a third part in thrall and the German capital in pawn; but West Germany's revival, her impressive economic achievements and successful incorporation into a powerful military alliance, were seen as a danger to these Soviet conquests. Particularly since the enviable prosperity of West Germany was all too easily visible at this time to the impoverished states behind the Iron Curtain, particularly East Germany. West Berlin had finally emerged as the 'shop-window of Western democracy' and the inevitable Soviet response was to demand that Berlin in the future be treated as fundamental to any proposed general agreement on Germany and furthermore that no peace conference on Germany could proceed without some agreement on arms control elsewhere. . . .

Khrushchev . . . was . . . committed to . . . a Communist take-over in West Germany as a necessary preliminary to unification.

Khrushchev . . . was . . . committed to . . . a Communist take-over in West Germany as a necessary preliminary to unification: 'What does the reunification of Germany mean under present conditions of existence of the two German states? On what basis could it be accomplished? The advocates of working class interests cannot even think of making the workers and peasants of the German Democratic Republic, who have set up a workers' and peasants' state and are successfully building Socialism, lose all their gains through reunification and agree to live as before in capitalist bondage.' The same message was being promulgated in Bonn [the capital of West Germany], where the Soviet Ambassador told a group of German political leaders that among the Soviet conditions for reunification were the following: 'major industry would have to be nationalized . . . the power of "monopoly capital" would have to be broken and the working class [i.e. the Communist Party] would have to assume political dominance.' Thus the creation of a strong pro-Western power in Central Europe was still seen by the Kremlin as a major threat, and it was to neutralise this that Khrushchev embarked upon a new diplomatic offensive, which was to last from 1957 to 1963.

Early Soviet Proposals

At first Soviet proposals embodied the twin concepts of neutrality and disengagement. Neutrality was envisaged as the successor of the demilitarization prescribed by [Joseph] Stalin [Soviet leader until 1953] at Potsdam in 1945; it was also a concept which benefited from the surviving residue of post-war fears and thus aimed at engaging the support of those in the West who still saw . . . the threat of revived German militarism. In 1957 Moscow produced its first positive proposal, a plan to create a neutral belt of states stretching from the far north of Europe through the heart of the continent, involving both Germanies, and southwards to the Mediterranean. This belt would consist of three distinct geographical entities. In the north a nuclear-free zone would be created in the Baltic, thus making it a 'sea of peace'. More controversial was the Soviet proposal for Central Europe; called the Rapacki Plan, after the Polish Foreign Minister, it envisaged a neutral and nuclear-free zone embracing Poland, Czechoslovakia and East and West Germany. In Southern Europe a Balkan Pact was suggested, on similar lines. At first the West took some interest in this Soviet blueprint for Europe and were inclined to accept their invitation to hold a summit conference to discuss it, particularly since the Rapacki Plan was projected as the first stage of a far-reaching scheme for disarmament in Central Europe. But eventually the entire proposal was rejected as an effort to consolidate Soviet dominance of Central and Eastern Europe. The central weakness of the plan was obvious: its creation of a no-man's-land in Central Europe, which would, like every previous demilitarized zone in history, sooner or later fall under the authority of its strongest neighbour.

However, Khrushchev was still determined to reach a solution to the German problem, so in 1958 he put pressure upon what he still regarded as the weak link of the Atlantic Alliance—the Western presence in Berlin. A victory over Berlin at this time would not only mean increased prestige for the entire Socialist camp but would also force the Western powers to accept the German Democratic Republic as no longer a mere Soviet satellite, . . . but as an equal nation. Such a victory would also result in the humiliation of Bonn and, by implication, NATO [the North Atlantic Treaty Organization]. Finally, it would be a triumph for the Khrushchev brand of 'peaceful co-existence', which involved paying lip-service to the *status quo* with the West while the Soviet 'system of society' exploited the nationalist awakening and social unrest in the world at large.

The Beginning of the Berlin Crisis

The Berlin crisis which culminated in the building of the Wall in 1961 can be said to have begun on 10 November 1958, with the first of Khrushchev's ultimatums concerning the city. He proposed that Berlin be reconstituted as a free city, in other words that all foreign troops be withdrawn, and stated in no uncertain terms that unless a settlement of the German question were negotiated within six months, Moscow would proceed with its own peace treaty with the DDR [German Democratic Republic]. The implications of this Soviet declaration were immediately apparent to the West: the superiority of the paramilitary forces of the DDR over the police forces of West Berlin would inevitably result in a merger of the two parts of the city. That Moscow ever seriously believed such a proposal would be accepted in the West can only be explained by their over-emphasis on the discord they believed was rife within NATO. For a short while their optimism was not unfounded. In his last few months as American Secretary of State [John Foster] Dulles was attracted to some parts of the Soviet plan, and suggested in press conferences that East Germany might be allowed a share of control over the access to West Berlin, and, even worse from Bonn's point of view, that the reunification of the two Germanies need not necessarily take place according to the hitherto-agreed Western formula of free elections as a first step. This attitude provoked a further outbreak of German-American tension, which even the personal visit of Dulles to Bonn in April 1959 did not completely resolve, and lingering fears of an American inclination to 'sell out' West Berlin to the Russians persisted in [the first chancellor of West Germany, Konrad] Adenauer's mind.

Britain also showed a positive reaction to the Soviet proposals. The British Prime Minister, Harold Macmillan, claimed to detect a genuine relaxation in international tension, and interpreted many domestic trends in the Soviet Union, towards material prosperity and internal stability, as something of a middle-class revolution under Communist labels and hence favourable for the West. He saw Khrushchev as a man honestly searching for peaceful solutions to outstanding problems and therefore deserving of at least a hearing. For this purpose in February 1959 he visited Moscow for ten days. Although Macmillan freely admitted in his memoirs that on most points at issue little agreement was reached, at least on the question of disengagement and Germany's rearmament there were signs of compromise. The final communiqué proposed further discussions towards establishing security in Central Europe by the limitation of arms both conventional and nuclear, on condition that a mutually acceptable and effective system of inspection could be set up.

Bonn was highly suspicious of this British optimism; Adenauer believed that Macmillan was by implication halfway towards recognizing the German Democratic Republic. In Moscow, Khrushchev was confident that he had at least caused a split in Western solidarity.

> *In 1958 [Khrushchev] put pressure upon what he still regarded as the weak link of the Atlantic Alliance—the Western presence in Berlin.*

Events soon proved both Adenauer's fears and Khrushchev's confidence equally unfounded. The subsequent conference of foreign ministers of the great powers, together with diplomatic representatives of the two Germanies, failed dismally, despite a summer of negotiation in Geneva. The West linked their proposals on Germany to an overall European security system, in order to overcome what they regarded as the central difficulty: military withdrawal while two hostile states, representing the respective political and military investments of each bloc, still faced one another in central Europe. Their suggestions failed because it would have been impossible to erect any European security system without incorporating East Germany, which they had already refused to do. The Soviet counter-proposal of a non-aggression treaty between NATO and the Warsaw

Pact also foundered on this Western refusal to recognize East Germany. Thus not only had the West doomed the Geneva meeting to failure but had further compromised their position over Berlin by allowing East German representatives into the negotiations. The West's dilemma was obvious: a solution of the Berlin question could now only be reached in terms of a *de facto* recognition of the East German régime.

Summit Preparations Go Well

In the autumn of 1959 Khrushchev visited the United States. Dulles was dead and his newly appointed successor, Christian A. Herter, had not had time to master his new office, a fact which did not go unnoticed by Khrushchev in this, the next round of his diplomatic offensive. While Khrushchev talked with Eisenhower at Camp David, the prospect of a deal between the super-powers caused much anxiety in Paris and Bonn. In the event, no specific promises on Berlin were made by either side, but the atmosphere of goodwill resulted in the decision to hold a summer meeting the following year. That spring Khrushchev made further preparations for the summit by paying a prolonged visit to France; the new French leader [Charles] De Gaulle was as yet an unknown quantity in his calculations. Neither German states had been invited to the summit, which suited Adenauer since it implied that the West did not wish to make any further gestures which might be interpreted as partial recognition of the German Democratic Republic. Khrushchev also felt that Adenauer's absence would be an advantage, since he regarded the German Chancellor as the main obstacle to a settlement of the Berlin question in Russia's favour.

The Western press . . . was speculating on the possible results of the failure of the talks long before the leaders ever met in Vienna.

In Paris Khrushchev indefatigably played on the traditional French fear of Germany; his constant theme, in speeches delivered both in the capital and throughout the provinces, was the devastation and atrocities that both France and Russia had suffered at the hands of the German

Europe During the Cold War

Denmark

Netherlands

Britain

Berlin

Belgium

East Germany

Poland

USSR

Luxembourg

West Germany

Czechoslovakia

Switzerland

Austria

Hungary

France

Italy

Romania

Yugoslavia

Spain

Soviet-Controlled Eastern Europe

Albania

invader. He appealed to that body of French opinion which saw the only means of insuring against a future German threat as being a close alliance with the Soviet Union. In a speech in Paris on 23 March, Khrushchev said: 'I believe that the German revenge-seekers are a bigger threat to France than to any other country . . . Now that militarism is being revived in Western Germany one must prevent a repetition of the errors of the past.' Although Khrushchev failed to win over De Gaulle, who stood firm on the Western pre-conditions for Berlin—respect for the *status quo* and free elections—he nevertheless left for home convinced that a large proportion of French public opinion had been won over to his views.

Vienna Summit a Failure

Such preparations by Khrushchev for the forthcoming talks made it imperative for the Western powers to work out a common policy on Berlin. De Gaulle's firmness allied with Adenauer's influence and Washington's disinclination now to yield the West's position determined the eventual policy: no substantial concessions to the Khrushchev proposals. Since the Berlin question was the main subject on the agenda, the summit was thus doomed before it began. The mood of pessimism throughout the foreign offices of the West communicated itself to the Western press, which was speculating on the possible results of the failure of the talks long before the leaders ever met in Vienna. A breakdown of negotiations would be a particularly hard blow for Khrushchev, who had not only initiated the conference but had also staked much of his own and his party's prestige on its successful outcome. The Russian leader's position within the Kremlin was at this time precarious and in particular opposition from the armed forces was becoming increasingly strong. They resented his interference in matters of strategic doctrine, and his emphasis on minimum deterrence meant that in a conflict situation the Soviet armed forces now had but a single option—nuclear war. Therefore, Khrushchev needed a positive agreement on Berlin at the summit talks if only to safeguard his own position at home and prove that his particular tactics were superior to any other 'Communist Course' and the best way of dealing with 'imperialists' such as the United States of America.

Khrushchev's difficulties within the Kremlin clearly dictated his behaviour over the U-2 Incident, which occurred just before the conference: an American high-altitude intelligence aircraft, the U-2, was shot down over Soviet territory and its pilot, Gary Powers, was subjected to the panoply of a Kremlin show trial. Khrushchev's tactics became clear when he demanded a full apology from Eisenhower; even if the Berlin question was not to be resolved in Russia's favour, at least the public discomfiture of an American president would be some compensation for the Soviet leadership. However, the Western reaction, particularly in the news media, was to support the Americans and play down the whole incident by putting it into its proper context, the normal processes of Cold War intelligence activities. Widespread espionage was conducted by both sides, as an important contribution to national security during the arms race. . . .

A Change in Soviet Foreign Policy

With the subsequent failure of the summit conference owing to deliberate sabotage by Khrushchev, Soviet foreign policy took on a new direction and emphasis. At first it was a difference in style rather than substance, a change in terminology, which nevertheless created the impression of a real war being planned. Khrushchev chose as his arena the United Nations, where his violent tirades seemed to herald a return to the hard-line days of Stalin. This post-summit trend in Soviet policy certainly produced side-effects, which were not all in accordance with Moscow's plans. Khrushchev had expected that his diplomatic offensive against the United States would result in renewed support and influence for Russia among the nations of the Third World. However, except in Cuba and the Congo, such benefits were not forthcoming, probably because his sabre-rattling threats of missile attack now perplexed those governments who had originally expressed confidence in Khrushchev's peaceful intentions.

The atmosphere of tension, and crises such as the U-2 affair, sapped the morale of the people of West Berlin; in their eyes, the Western powers had demonstrated that under the threat of nuclear war not only could they not devise any positive alternative to the *status quo* in the city, but that they did not even consider it feasible to hold Berlin indefinitely against mounting Soviet pressure. In East Germany, [East German leader Walter] Ulbricht was becoming restive and the West Berliners were fully aware that the continued refusal of either side to force a showdown over Berlin might well leave the field clear for the East German leader to act independently. His own régime was still desperately weak, which fact alone might tempt him into some rash action. The plight of Ulbricht's government, and its unpopularity amongst the East Germans, was fully appreciated by Khrushchev, and many of his actions in the autumn of 1960 and the following spring were conditioned as much by this circumstance as by the need to mollify the Kremlin. For Khrushchev, the only way in which East Germany could avoid a repetition of the 1953 uprising was by securing control over both parts of Berlin. This assertion was supported by the serious political difficulties experienced by the satellite, the shabbiest of all Communist enterprises in Eastern Europe. As long as a free West Berlin existed as a shop window for the material benefits of Western capitalist society and as long as the city provided so convenient an escape route for the East German, then the consolidation of Communism in East Germany remained in doubt. The sheer loss in manpower through West Berlin was partly the motivation behind Khrushchev's urgent demands in 1961 for an end to the anomalous situation in Berlin. Authoritative sources in Bonn estimated that in the ten years of the Ulbricht régime more than four million East Germans had made their way to the West via West Berlin—almost a quarter of the total population. What was even more significant was the nature of these refugees: most were young and many came from the élite professions of teaching, medicine and technology. Although the initial time-limit set by Khrushchev in June 1959 for a negotiated settlement of the German question had long since come and gone, it was still his declared aim to stabilize East Germany by making Berlin its capital by any means short of war or the risk of war; but he was fast running out of options.

Khrushchev Meets with Kennedy

On 4 June 1961 Khrushchev met the new US President, John F. Kennedy, at Vienna and presented him with what might be termed an *aide-mémoire* [an outline of important items of a proposed agreement] on the question of a peace treaty for Germany. This document contained three main proposals: the first suggested that the Germans should be given six months to agree on a method of reunification, and if they then had still failed to reach a settlement, then the four powers should sign separate peace treaties with the two German states; secondly, West Berlin should become a free city and completely demilitarized; finally, all questions of access to Berlin should be decided through direct negotiations with the German Democratic Republic. Khrushchev emphasized in subsequent speeches that the Soviet Union would sign a separate peace treaty with the East Germans if the Western governments refused an all-German treaty: 'The Soviet Union and all other peace-loving countries will do all that they can so that it is signed by the end of the year.'

Here the Kremlin reverted to the setting of a time-limit over Berlin. The previous one had been allowed to be exceeded because of the proximity of the summit conference, but now that the meetings had occurred and international differences over Berlin were seen to be as wide as ever, the Russians felt that the only way in which they could make the West modify their position was by the use of threat.

The Kennedy response was immediate and dramatic. In a speech on 25 July 1961 he said: 'I have said that West Berlin is militarily untenable. And so was Bastogne. And so in fact was Stalingrad. Any dangerous spot is tenable if men—brave men—will make it so.' This was a somewhat unrealistic statement, since Berlin was and still is [in 1973] militarily completely untenable; the only effective defence of the city is the threat of thermo-nuclear war, since it could never be held by conventional ground forces. Nevertheless, Kennedy placed a new emphasis on such conventional forces by increasing the overall strength of US combat divisions by 200,000 men and allocating a further $2,000 million for conventional weapons and civil defence. An additional 40,000 men were flown in as reinforcements to the US Seventh Army in Germany, while at the same time both Britain and France brought some of their units up to combat strength. The West Germans responded by delaying the release date for many of the conscripts in the Bundeswehr [German Federal Armed Forces].

By August 1961 the atmosphere in Central Europe was electric, and there was a marked increase in the number of refugees who fled from the East into Berlin.

Kennedy's speeches and the overt military preparations of that summer had an important influence on American domestic politics. By increasing the draft, calling up reserve formations, and above all by focusing attention on Civil Defence, Kennedy brought home to the American people the seriousness of the crisis. And while Khrushchev increased Soviet military strength in East Germany to counter the NATO build-up, the significance of the American moves was obvious: Kennedy was determined to hold on to West Berlin, even if it meant war.

The Construction of the Wall

By August 1961 the atmosphere in Central Europe was electric, and there was a marked increase in the number of refugees who fled from the East into Berlin. At the same time a number of significant initiatives came from the West aimed at de-escalating the crisis. To the dismay of Adenauer and Bonn, influential voices in the American Senate, particularly Senators Mansfield and Fulbright, called for Western recognition of the German Democratic Republic. Another popular proposal at the time was that the United Nations Organization be moved from New York to the Charlottenburg. However, such suggestions were soon made irrelevant by Ulbricht's ensuing actions: whether he was backed by the Russians or not has never been established, but he began a new campaign of intimidation against the *Grenzgänger* (Western citizens who worked in East Berlin) and raised tension to crisis pitch. Rumours began to circulate in West Berlin and the Federal Republic that Ulbricht was planning to close the frontiers and a supposedly secret meeting of the Warsaw Pact powers in Moscow in early August seemed to lend substance to such speculation. By now, an average of 1,500 people a day were crossing into West Berlin; meanwhile, Western Intelligence plotted the movement of Soviet units around the city itself.

In the early hours of Sunday, 13 August, squads of East German workers erected makeshift wire barriers and fences along the line of demarcation across the city, while at the same time the underground railway and municipal train services which operated across the sectors came to a halt. The first stage of the isolation of West Berlin had been completed.

The construction of the Berlin Wall was very much a logical development in post-war European politics.

The construction of the Berlin Wall was very much a logical development in post-war European politics. The Berlin crisis was hourly increasing the risks of a head-on clash between the super-powers, and West Berlin's open invitation to refugees only exacerbated the situation. The only other means of preventing the movement of refugees would be to organize a vast network of police and troops around the eastern approaches to the city; however, such a cordon would be inefficient and in any case could only be operated for short periods. The construction of a barrier and the control of crossing-points represented the most logical solution to the problem, at the same time demonstrating Khrushchev's desire to separate the two crises, the abnormal circumstances of Berlin from the question of a divided Germany. The closure of the frontier was felt in Moscow to increase the chances of Western recognition of the Democratic Republic.

The Criticism of Western Inaction

The governments of the West have since been criticized at home for not reacting immediately to stop the Wall being built; it certainly caught them by surprise, being a development which had apparently never been contemplated even by the experts on crisis management. It was a flagrant breach of the Four-Power Status on Berlin because although thirteen crossing points were left open to allow Allied forces to move in East Berlin, in practical terms it meant that East Berlin was finally integrated, by unilateral action, into the German Democratic Republic. But the use of actual force would be dangerous and Khrushchev, in common with the Western leaders, knew very well that he could make no moves against West Berlin without incurring the counter-threat of thermo-nuclear war; for the very same reason, however, he was free to do whatever he wished over East Berlin. The Soviet leader was at great pains to emphasise that the building of the Wall did not in any way threaten the integrity of the Western presence, either through pressure on access routes or by a direct threat to West Berlin, but was rather a punitive move against East Berlin. Nevertheless morale was badly shaken in West Berlin and Bonn, and the usual gossip circulated to the effect that the West had in fact long known about the plan. The people of Berlin and West Germany hence felt that the Allied commitment to protect them had been seriously undermined; a feeling which fortunately soon passed. Positive military action would have been foolhardy anyway, simply because the Communists had such overwhelming superiority in local armed forces; even if the West had moved in and torn up the barriers, the East Germans would then have erected them inside their own territory, which would have involved the West in a violation of sovereignty if they had attempted to pull the obstacles down a second time.

It must be stressed that the Soviet stake in this dispute was much greater than that of the Western powers, being nothing less than her own credibility in the eyes of the German Democratic Republic. The survival of the Ulbricht régime was dependent on the presence of Russian armed forces and if the Kremlin had shown that it would allow the Western powers to determine how they should use this force, the result might well have been the East German population displaying open resistance to their government. Hence, any Western demand for the demolition of the wire obstacles, even at this early stage, would have provoked a challenge to the East German régime, which would thus have greatly increased the risk of conflict. The Soviet Union had allowed the closure of the city in circumstances that were the most favourable possible to the West, and any counter-move by the West, no matter how local or how limited, could well have resulted in a threat to their own access routes, a situation which would have left the West with no option but to escalate the confrontation.

At first there was no great interference in the movement of West Berliners across the new frontier; this did not occur until 23 August, when the wire was replaced by the permanent ugliness of a wall and there was a gradual reduction in the number of access points. Many commentators have pointed out this time-lag between the initial appearance of the wire and the eventual construction of the Wall and suggested that if the West had made a move against the former then the Communists would have thought twice about building the latter. Although it does seem that the total acquiescence of the Western authorities to the initial barrier might well have encouraged Ulbricht to turn the wire into concrete and impose further restrictions on movement, the facts of the case were that the Soviet Union held all the cards, unless the West wished to invoke the threat of nuclear retaliation. Even a carefully-limited Western resistance ran the risk of a Soviet 'over-response' and the Wall was simply not worth that risk.

3

The Construction of the Wall Alleviated East-West Tensions

Richard Reeves

In reflecting on the Cold War ten years after the fall of the Berlin Wall, Richard Reeves outlines his reasons for believing that the building of the Berlin Wall prevented a nuclear war between the Americans and the Soviets.

Just after World War II, Germany and Berlin were divided into zones controlled by the United States, France, and England in the West and the Soviet Union in the East. In 1961, the residents of Communist-controlled East Germany were fleeing to the democratic West in numbers up to three thousand per day. To stem this exodus, the Communists might have had to use military force. If the Communists chose this route, it was the policy of the United States to use its arsenal—including nuclear weapons—in response. Such an event would most probably have prompted a third world war.

Reeves asserts that President Kennedy was not surprised by the building of the wall as a way to prevent the migration from East Germany. Indeed, Reeves claims Kennedy was relieved, for once this flight was stopped, the threat of military action was alleviated. Richard Reeves is the author of twelve books, including *President Kennedy: Profile of Power*. He is a syndicated columnist and has written for the *New York Times*, the *New Yorker*, and *Esquire*.

Richard Reeves, "How the Wall Prevented World War 3," *The Star-Ledger*, November 15, 1999, p. 15. Copyright © 1999 by *The Star-Ledger*. Reproduced by permission.

The fireworks and music marking the 10th anniversary of the fall of the Berlin Wall were certainly justified as a dramatic symbol of the collapse of the Soviet empire and the end of the Cold War. But we should celebrate, too, the building of the wall, beginning on Aug. 13, 1961. That cruel division of Berlin into two cities was possibly the single action that prevented nuclear war between the United States and the Soviet Union.

If there were to have been a nuclear world war, it would have begun not in Korea or Cuba or Vietnam. The trigger would have been pulled in Europe, where Americans and our allies confronted the armies of communism led by the Soviets.

A wall, a divided Berlin, in fact, was what Kennedy wanted.

The Communists' problem was that East Germans were fleeing west through the open border between East and West Berlin at a rate that reached more than 3,000 a day in that summer of 1961. The best and the brightest of the East, the young and the educated, the engineers, doctors and teachers, were escaping impoverished totalitarianism. Our problem was that the Communists might choose to move militarily to solve their problem by taking over West Berlin, an enclave 110 miles inside East Germany. In that island in a Red sea, under the agreements that ended World War II, there were only 15,000 American, British and French troops, surrounded by dozens of divisions of the Red Army.

If the Soviets decided on a military solution, they could have blocked the road and rail line to West Germany and taken West Berlin in 24 hours, taken all of Germany in a couple of weeks and all of Western Europe in a couple of months. Unless . . .

Unless the Americans used nuclear weapons to stop them. U.S. policy was to use nuclear weapons in that case—and presumably the Soviets would have retaliated in kind.

A Great Victory?

"West Berlin," said President John F. Kennedy, "has become—as never before—the great testing place of Western courage and will. . . . We are clear about what must be done—and we intend to do it. . . . An attack on West Berlin will be regarded as an attack on all of us. . . . We shall not surrender." He said that on Aug. 3, 1961—in public.

In private, Kennedy said of Soviet leader Nikita Khrushchev, "This is intolerable for Khrushchev. East Germany is hemorrhaging to death. The entire East bloc is in danger. He has to do something to stop this. Perhaps a wall. And there's not a damn thing we can do about it."

A wall, a divided Berlin, in fact, was what Kennedy wanted—though God knows he could not say that in public without risking impeachment or a disastrous defeat in the 1964 election. He had to talk and act tough.

The erection of the wall was not the great surprise we present it as now. Among many other public discussions of the possibility was a cover story in the *Reporter* magazine on March 16, 1961, which Kennedy read, that said: "The only way to stop refugees is to seal off both East Berlin and the Soviet Zone by total physical security measures . . . Khrushchev will ring down the Iron Curtain in front of East Berlin—with searchlights and machine gun towers, barbed wire and police dog patrols. . . . The West's main problem is to provide some way out for the Soviets with little loss of face . . ."

That is exactly what happened five months later. The wall was built, legally so to speak, totally in East German territory. If we had wanted to knock it down, allied troops would have to have crossed the line, invading the Eastern zone. When Kennedy heard the first news of East German troops stringing barbed wire, he went sailing. He did not comment for more than 24 hours.

In private, he said, "This is the end of the Berlin crisis. . . . They're not going to overrun Berlin." The wall was a great victory for Kennedy, but of course no American leader could say that until it fell 30 years later.

Chapter **3**

The Fall of the Berlin Wall and the Consequences for Berlin

1

Berliners Celebrate the Destruction of the Berlin Wall

Andreas Ramos

In his personal account of the events of November 11 and 12, 1989, Andreas Ramos describes the people and events he witnessed at the fall of the Berlin Wall.

Ramos began his journey in Denmark, driving thirteen hours to Berlin through the newly opened East German border checkpoints. He and his family joined the thousands of East and West Germans celebrating in the streets of Berlin.

On Thursday, the 9th of November, 1989, and Friday the 10th, the TV and radio in Denmark was filled with news about the events in Berlin. The Wall was about to fall. On Saturday morning, the 11th of November, I heard on the radio that East Germany was collapsing. At the spur of the moment, I suggested to Karen, my Danish wife, and two Danish friends, Rolf Reitan and Nana Kleist, that we should go to Berlin. We talked about what one should take to a revolution: it was a very cold, dry November day. We settled on a dozen boiled eggs, a thermos pot of coffee, extra warm clothes, sleeping bags, and a battery-powered radio. The four of us packed into my 25 year old Volkswagen bug and we drove off.

It's normally an eight hour drive from Aarhus, Denmark, to Berlin. We took the Autobahn down to Hamburg and then across one of the transit routes to Berlin. Berlin is in the center of East Germany. There are only three highways which allow access from West Germany. At the border city of Braunschweig (Brunswick), on the German side, we began to see the first Trabants. These are small East German cars. They don't just look like toy cars, they look like Donald Duck's car. It was designed by a famous East German industrial designer during the 50s and it never changed. It's the only car in the world with tail fins. It has cheap, thin metal that rusts easily. The two-stroke engine buzzes like a lawn mower and pumps out clouds of smoke. God help you if you're standing near one. Trabants, which Germans call Trabis, have a top speed of about 50 miles an hour.

After a pizza in Braunschweig, we drove towards the German/German border. It was about 11 P.M. at night now. The traffic began to slow down. Soon there was very heavy traffic. In the distance there was a tremendous cloud of light. No one knew what was going on. On the radio, reports followed one another, contradicting each other. Soon, we began to pass cars that were parked along both sides of the Autobahn. People were walking along, all heading towards the border.

The East German Border

We finally reached the border just after midnight. The East German border was always a serious place. Armed guards kept you in your car, watching for attempts at escapes. Tonight was a different country. Over 20,000 East and West Germans were gathered there in a huge party: as each Trabi came through, people cheered and clapped. East Germans drove through the applause, grinning, dazed, as thousands of flashbulbs went off. The traffic jam was spectacular. The cloud of light turned out to be the headlights of tens of thousands of cars in a huge cloud of Trabi exhaust fumes. We got out of the car and began walking. Between lanes of cars, streams of people were walking, talking together. Under one light, a group of musicians were playing violins and accordions and men and women were dancing in circles. Despite the brilliantly cold night, car windows were open and everyone talked to each other.

We met people from Belgium, France, Sweden, Spain, England: they had all left their homes and come to see the wall be torn down. Germans were drunk with joy. Everyone spoke in all sorts of languages and half languages. French spoke German and Spaniards spoke French and everyone spoke a bit of German. We walked for a while with a French family from Belgium: the mother had packed her two young daughters into the car and came to see the German revolution.

Along with everyone else headed towards Berlin were thousands of East Germans; they had been in West Europe for a blitz tour with the kids and grandmother in the back, to look around and drive back again. Without passports, they had simply driven through the borders. Amused West European border guards let them pass. They smiled and waved to everyone.

Under one light, a group of musicians were playing violins and accordions and men and women were dancing in circles.

At the checkpoint, which is a 25 lane place, people milled around. It was nearly 3 A.M. by now. It had taken us three hours to go through the traffic jam of cheering and applause. West Germans are environmentally conscious and if they're stuck in traffic, they turn off the engine and push their cars. East Germans, on the other hand, sat in their Trabis, putting out clouds of exhaust. Everyone had their radios on and everywhere was music. People had climbed up into trees, signs, buildings, everything, to wave and shout. Television teams stood around filming everything. People set up folding tables and were handing out cups of coffee. A Polish engineer and his wife had run out of gas; someone gave us some rope, so we tied the rope to his car and pulled them along.

We walked through the border. On both sides the guard towers were empty and the barbed wire was shoved aside in great piles. Large signs told us that we needed sets of car documents. The East German guard asked if we had documents. I handed him my Danish cat's vaccination documents, in Danish. He waved us through.

We were finally inside East Germany on the transit highway to Berlin. We could see headlights stretching into the distance, a river of light winding through hills and valleys as far as one could see. We counted our odometer and saw that in the opposite direction both lanes were filled and stopped for 35 kilometers. We counted people and cars for a kilometer and guessed that perhaps another one hundred thousand people were headed westward towards West Germany.

We drove along, listening to the radio. The only thing was Berlin. Reporters went back and forth, describing the events on the streets and where people had gathered at the wall. There were reports of shoving and arrests. Large crowds were beginning to form into mobs. Police stood around. There were reports of rumor of soldiers and military vehicles, both East and West. At one point in the wall, the crowd had begun to tear down the wall. They succeeded in carrying away a 3 meter tall slab.

The Arrival in Berlin

We arrived in Berlin at 4:30 A.M., five hours longer than usual. We drove first to Brandenburgerplatz, where the statute of Winged Victory stands atop a 50 meter column, which celebrates a military victory in the 1890s over Denmark. Cars were abandoned everywhere, wherever there was space. Over 5,000 people were there. I began talking to people. We left the car and began to walk through a village of television trucks, giant satellite dishes, emergency generators, and coils of cables, and tents. Cameramen slept under satellite dishes. At the wall, West German police and military was lined up to prevent chaos. West German military trucks were lined up against the wall, to protect it from the West Germans. Hundreds of West German police stood in rows with their tall shields. On top of the wall, lined up at parade rest, stood East German soldiers with their rifles. Groups of West Germans stood around fires that they had built. No one knew what was going on.

After a while, we walked to Potsdammer Platz. This used to be the center of Berlin. All traffic once passed through the Potsdammer Platz. Now it was a large empty field, bisected by the wall. Nearby was the mound that was the remains of Hitler's bunker, from which he commanded Germany into total defeat. We talked to Germans and many said that the next break in the wall would be here. It was still very dark and cold at 5 A.M. Perhaps 7,000 people were pressed together, shouting, cheering, clapping. We pushed through the crowd. From the East German side we could hear the sound of heavy machines. With a giant drill, they were punching holes in the wall. Every time a drill poked through, everyone cheered. The banks of klieg lights would come on. People shot off fireworks and emergency flares and rescue rockets. Many were using hammers to chip away at the wall. There were countless holes. At one place, a crowd of East German soldiers looked through a narrow hole. We reached through and shook hands. They couldn't see the crowd so they asked us what was going on and we described the scene for them. Someone lent me a hammer and I knocked chunks of rubble from the wall, dropping several handfuls into my pocket. The wall was made of cheap, brittle concrete: the Russians had used too much sand and water.

We could hear the sound of heavy machines. With a giant drill, they were punching holes in the wall. Every time a drill poked through, everyone cheered.

Progress seemed rather slow and we figured it'd take another hour. The car wouldn't start anymore without a push. We went back towards the city for coffee or beer or whatever. We drove down the Kurfurstendamm (the Ku'-damm), the central boulevard. Hundreds of thousands of people were walking around, going in and out of stores, looking around, drinking cheap East German champagne. Thousands of champagne bottles littered the streets. Thousands of Trabis were parked wherever they had found a space, between trees, between park benches, on traffic islands. Everything was open: restaurants, bars, discos, everything. Yesterday over two million East Germans had entered Berlin. The radio reported that over 100,000 were entering every hour. With Berlin's population of three million, there were over five million people milling around in delirious joy celebrating the reunion of the city after 21 years. A newspaper wrote banner headlines: Germany is reunited in the streets!

The East German government was collapsing. East German money was worthless. West Germany gave every East German 100 Deutschmark, which amounted to several months wages. The radio announced that banks and post offices would open at 9 A.M. so that the people could pick up their cash with a stamp in their identification papers. Thousands stood in line.

We left our car in front of the Gedankniskirchen, the Church of Remembrance, a bombed out ruins of a church, left as a memorial to the victims of the war.

A Joyous Celebration

We walked into a bar. Nearly everything was sold out. A huge crowd was talking and laughing all at once. We found a table. An old woman came up and asked if we were Germans. We said no, Danish, and invited her and her family to our table. We shared chairs and beer. They were East Germans, mother, father, and daughter. She worked in a factory, her husband was a plumber, and the daughter worked in a shop. They came from a small village several hundred kilometers to the south. The old woman said that she had last seen Berlin 21 years ago and couldn't recognize it. They told us about the chaos of the last few weeks. I asked them what they had bought in Berlin. They all pulled out their squirt guns. They thought it was so funny to fill up the squirt guns with beer and shoot at everybody. The family had chased a cat in an alley and eaten a dinner of bananas, a luxury for them. We talked about movies; they knew the directors and cameramen. The father was very happy at the idea of being able to travel. He wanted to go to Peru and see Machu Picchu and then to Egypt and see the pyramids. They had no desire to live in the West. They knew about unemployment and drug problems. Their apartment rent was $2 a month. A bus ticket cost less than a penny.

I saw an indescribable joy in people's faces. It was the end of the government telling people what not to do, it was the end of the Wall, the war, the East, the West.

At seven A.M. or so, we left and headed back to the Potsdammer Platz. Old Volkswagens don't have gas gauges. The car ran out of gas. Someone said that there was a gas station five blocks ahead. People joined us in pushing the car to the gas station. When we arrived, people were standing around.

The electricity had failed in the neighborhood so the gas pumps were dead. The owner shrugged at the small bother and waved us towards the coffee. Dozens of East Germans, young, old, children, stood around drinking coffee. After an hour or so, the electricity came on and we filled up the tank. With a crowd of people, we pushed the car up and down the street three times to get it to start. We drove back to Potsdammer Platz.

Everything was out of control. Police on horses watched. There was nothing they could do. The crowd had swollen. People were blowing long alpine horns which made a huge noise. There were fireworks, kites, flags and flags and flags, dogs, children. The wall was finally breaking. The cranes lifted slabs aside. East and West German police had traded caps. To get a better view, hundreds of people were climbing onto a shop on the West German side. We scampered up a nine foot wall. People helped each other; some lifted, others pulled. All along the building, people poured up the wall. At the Berlin Wall itself, which is 3 meters high, people had climbed up and were sitting astride. The final slab was moved away. A stream of East Germans began to pour through. People applauded and slapped their backs. A woman handed me a giant bottle of wine, which I opened and she and I began to pour cups of wine and hand them to the East Germans. Journalists and TV reporters struggled to hold their cameras. A foreign news agency's van with TV cameras on top was in a crowd of people; it rocked and the cameramen pleaded with the crowd. Packed in with thousands, I stood at the break in the wall. Above me, a German stood atop the wall, at the end, balanced, waving his arms and shouting reports to the crowd. With all of the East Germans coming into West Berlin, we thought it was only fair that we should go to East Berlin. A counterflow started. Looking around, I saw an indescribable joy in people's faces. It was the end of the government telling people what not to do, it was the end of the Wall, the war, the East, the West. If East Germans were going west, then we should go east, so we poured into East Berlin. Around me, people spoke German, French, Polish, Russian, every language. A woman handed her camera to someone who was standing atop rubble so that he could take her picture. I passed a group of American reporters; they didn't speak anything and couldn't understand what was going on, pushing their microphones into people's faces, asking "Do you speak English?" Near me, a knot of people cheered as the mayors of East Berlin and West Berlin met and shook hands. I stood with several East German guards, their rifles slung over their shoulders. I asked them if they had bullets in those things. They grinned and said no. From some houses, someone had set up loudspeakers and played Beethoven's ninth symphony: Alle Menschen werden Bruder. All people become brothers. On top of every building were thousands of people. Berlin was out of control. There was no more government, neither in East nor in West. The police and the army were helpless. The soldiers themselves were overwhelmed by the event. They were part of the crowd. Their uniforms meant nothing. The Wall was down.

After a while, we left and went back to the city, to find some food. The TV was set to East German TV. The broadcasters began showing whatever they wanted: roving cameras in the street, film clips, porno, speeches from parliament, statements, videos, nature films, live interviews. West Berliners went out of their homes and brought East Germans in for food and rest. A friend of ours in Berlin had two families sleeping in her living room. The radio told that in Frankfurt, a Trabi had been hit by a Mercedes. Nothing happened to the Mercedes but the Trabi was destroyed. A crowd of people collected money for the East German family; the driver of the Mercedes gave them her keys and lent them her car for the weekend. A West German went home, got his truck, and drove the Trabi back to East Germany. Late Sunday, the West German government declared on radio and TV that East Germans had free access to all public transportation: buses, streetcars, and trains, plus free admission to all zoos, museums, concerts, practically everything. More than 80% of East Germany was on vacation in West Germany, nearly 13 million people, visiting family and friends in the West. After a week, nearly all returned home.

After a dinner of spaghetti, we got back into the Volkswagen and headed home. The radio talked about delays of ten hours, but then again, that was just another rumor. At the border, there were no guards anymore. Late the next morning, we were back in Denmark.

2

The Fall of the Berlin Wall Creates Confusion and Euphoria for Berliners

Christopher Hope

In this account of Berlin written just after the wall fell, Christopher Hope compares Berlin before and after the destruction of the wall that divided it. Hope characterizes a divided Berlin as schizophrenic, a "distant theater of the cold war." However, when the wall came down, Berlin became a much different city: celebratory, open, and welcoming.

In his walk through Berlin, Hope also noted the confusion and worry displayed on the faces of some West Berliners who still consider the East Berliners—the "Ossies"—as "different." Lastly, Hope comments on the unremarkable condition of East Berlin streets and buildings after twenty-eight years under Communist control. Christopher Hope is an acclaimed South African writer and poet currently residing in England.

You know that things are serious when the TV news stations start flying in their anchor men and women. Chattering groups of them thronged Berlin Airport when I arrived on November 12, father figures and mother confessors from the news desks of the American networks, the British Broadcasting Corp., Japanese TV, and the European pop and sports satellite channels. They were eager to pre-

Christopher Hope, "Seeing Is Believing: In Berlin, the 'Ossies' Go West," *The New Republic*, vol. 201, December 18, 1989, pp. 14–17. Copyright © 1989 by The New Republic, Inc. Reproduced by permission.

sent the news in situ, beside the Berlin Wall, in front of the Brandenburg Gate. They were attended by baggage bearers, drones, and soldiers who formed a kind of protective scrimmage, easing their costly charges through passport control, incredulous that mere officials should obstruct the faces welcomed into millions of homes each night.

Berliners have always displayed disrespect when faced with power or privilege. And household names become very parochial the moment they leave the house. The famous faces, it must be said, are paler than expected, the eyes flutter restlessly as if searching for makeup and the auto-cue. As the Berliners well knew, these were people who a few weeks ago could not have picked out their divided city on a map. Berlin flickered in the memory, if at all, mixed with images of Liza Minnelli belting out her stuff in Cabaret. Indeed, for most people Berlin was an improbable oasis in the East German wilderness, cut in two by the Wall, surrounded by Russian troops, a stump of a city crowded with allied soldiers, spiked with missiles, lined with steak houses.

A Divided Berlin

Berlin was last in the news in a big way during the Berlin airlift, and the building of the Wall in 1961. It featured vividly when President Kennedy gazed out across the Wall and proclaimed: "I am a Berliner." But thereafter it was simply a schizophrenic city. A remnant of a vanished metropolis, occupied by its conquerors; in the West a prosperous fortress of two million people; in the East a prison house its masters called paradise, a place of outer darkness. Berlin was not a place—it was an issue. It never quite seemed to be part of modern Germany. When people thought of West Germany they tended to think of Bonn, the apologetic federal capital, of Mercedes and BMW, and of the strength of the deutsche mark [German currancy]. It was devoutly to be hoped that the two Germanys would one day be reunited, but outside the circles of the devout, no one was putting any money on it.

Since the erection of the Wall [in 1961], Berlin has become a kind of distant theater of the cold war. A fine place for spy stories, the scene of memorable exchanges of secret agents; daring escapes by hugely brave men and women hidden in the cunning compartments of trucks and automobiles; flights by hot air balloon; midnight dashes through the sewers beneath the city. And of abortive escapes that ended in gunfire and bleeding bodies. Along the length of the Wall small tabernacles remember with a name or a photograph those who did not get away.

The Night the Wall Fell

When suddenly the world was stood on its head. The night of Friday, November 10, the East Germans began smashing through the Wall. By November 14 there were 22 new crossing points, with promises of more to come. And through these gaps poured the grateful tens of thousands. The invasion so long predicted was coming true. Even the direction was right—the invaders came from the East. But they carried not rifles but shopping bags, and they arrived not in tanks but on foot, or in tiny two-stroke motorcars called Trabants, belching fumes, their fiberglass frames shivering on their uncertain chassis. To watch the tiny Trabant cross the Wall and go chugging along the broad West Berlin boulevards, impatiently followed by a gas-guzzling, absurdly fast turbo triumph of German automotive engineering, is to be present at a motorized street theater. The way into the future might be summed up by a single stage direction: "Exit a Trabant, pursued by a Porsche."

And what on earth was one to make of a German people who . . . were no longer preparing for the war but mounting shopping expeditions instead?

West Berliners, usually so laconic, acerbic, irreverent, melted in the face of this invasion. The Opera House offered free performances of Mozart's Magic Flute. The city fathers allowed free travel on the subway, the U-Bahn. They gave each new arrival 100 marks to spend. The department stores hung out welcome signs and exchanged the visitors' dud currency at the rate of ten East German marks for one West German mark. Around the square at the top of the Kurfurstendamm [a West Berlin thoroughfare], beside the ruins of the Kaiser Wilhelm Memorial Church commemorating the destruction of Berlin, sausage stalls appeared, trestle tables, beakers of beer, mobile toilets, street musicians, and unbounded conviviality. The visitors were quickly dubbed the "Ossies" to distinguish them from the West Berliners, who became, naturally, the "Wessies." When Ossies met Wessies, there took place in West Berlin the biggest damn family re-union Europe has seen since the War.

True, there were also a few party poopers about. Taxi drivers worried aloud about the cost of it all. After all, there were at least 1.2 million East Berliners (or had been the last time anyone had been brave enough or foolhardy enough to count them), and at 100 marks a head, the overall subsidy for this invasion, in every sense, was not small beer. Similarly, guest workers employed to do the work that West Berliners disdain took a rather dim view. "What will happen to me?" the Turkish cleaning attendant of a block of flats asked her employer, "when the Ossies undercut me?" Her employer appeared happily unconcerned. "I know. I've had three offers already."

And what of the thousands of troops that the Western allies and the Russians have kept massed along this crucial border? More worrying still, to the Poles and others—with sad memories of the last united Germany—where were the borders of Germany itself? Why had the West German chancellor, on a visit to Poland, declined to state that the postwar boundaries were immovable? And what on earth was one to make of a German people who, it seemed, were no longer preparing for the war but mounting shopping ex-peditions instead?

It was all very confusing and very euphoric and vaguely troubling all at once. Anyone who imagined that things would settle down did not, as they say in Berlin, have all his cups in the cupboard.

A Symbol of the War

Such people also mistook the significance of symbols. A Wall had once stood between East and West, built of stone and stained with blood. One night, without warning, it fell down. And only the rich bird life, thriving along its empty, eerie length, would mourn its passing. No one was surprised by the news that three Communist mayors from the East had committed suicide. It was the opinion of otherwise pa-cific matrons taking coffee in the Kempinski Eck, the fa-mous plush, glass-fronted observatory on the Kurfursten-damm, that the disgraced former leader of East Germany,

Erich Honecker, "do the decent thing" and follow suit. West Berliners have always detested the Wall, but they learned to live with it. They have jogged along its length and have daubed it with graffiti from end to end, but except on rare occasions when it thrust itself into view with a spectacular escape, or some important politician came to call and made a speech, they forgot about it. What West Berlin has never allowed anybody to forget is the War itself. Bullet holes are still to be seen, spattering the sides of buildings. Fragments of the portals of the old Berlin synagogue are cemented into the porch of the Jewish Community Center in Fasanenstrasse [a side street of the Kurfurstendamm]. West Berlin is a city loud with ghosts. The area around the Wall added to the sense of wartorn desolation. Once it was the site of the Potsdamer Platz, among the busiest intersections in Europe, the very heart of Berlin. Since the War ended it has been a muddy, disconsolate slum. Taxi drivers assured visitors with laconic understatement that it was not "a development area." The deserted embassies look like the victims of some below-stairs revolt by the lower vegetable orders. Creepers [vines] spread across their facades and reach through open windows into empty rooms.

It must be strange to ask directions from a man who a week earlier would have shot you for trying to leave the country.

Reminders of the cataclysm are everywhere: the Hitler bunker; the site of the Gestapo torture chambers in Wilhelmstrasse; the fragmentary remains of the old Anhalter station, a crumbling facade and a few headless statues on a roof out of which trees have sprouted. Before the War the Anhalter dispatched 60 trains a day to Dresden, Rome, Vienna. Nearby is Friedrichstrasse [a once-busy street in Berlin], now a gray shadow of its pre-war, tinselly self. It sputters out in a pizzeria and a rash of bars, ending abruptly when it runs up against Checkpoint Charlie. The graffiti on the Wall reveals the genial derision in which West Berliners hold the foreigner's tender fascination with this monstrous monument: "What are you staring at? Have you never seen a wall before?"

There has always been something inconsolably sad in

the air of West Berlin. East Berlin, by contrast, has always pretended otherwise. East Berliners never spoke of their city as "East Berlin," but always and only as Berlin, the capital of the only legitimate Germany. They preferred to ignore the existence of the imposter stuck away in the middle of 110 miles of East German territory. East German soldiers were to be seen regularly changing the guard Unter Den Linden, still doing the goose step, wearing helmets like soup plates.

Crossing into East Berlin

Naturally I crossed the Wall into the East for the simple pleasure of witnessing East Germans moving the other way. They waited patiently in long lines, helped by the border guards to fill in their travel forms. It must be strange to ask directions from a man who a week earlier would have shot you for trying to leave the country. It must have been even stranger for the guards themselves trained to snarl, shoot, and inspect the undersides of tourist buses with giant dentist mirrors. Overnight they had become part of the courtesy staff, obliging, efficient, seemingly delighted that most of the population planned a trip abroad.

I traveled to the East with a British novelist who had never made the crossing before. She had a theory that you could tell you were getting older when the popes started looking younger. But in Berlin, that test seemed really to apply to border guards. They appeared to have shed years overnight. "Please step this way to exchange your money," a smiling fellow invited toothily, holding the door. Only those used to making this dreary crossing would understand the novelty of his demeanor. I exchanged good West German marks for bad, an obligatory transfer, a tax on curiosity. One day East German banknotes will, like the Wall itself, become collectors' items. On the face of the 20 mark note [German writer and poet Johann] Goethe stares back guiltily, as if disturbed to find himself so framed.

There has never been much to see in the streets of East Berlin, or in the shops. A smart new coffeehouse adorns the corner of Friedrichstrasse, in its continuation on the other side of the Wall. It is always packed to capacity. Most of the customers appear to have taken up their seats soon after the building was completed and show no signs of leaving. In a nearby supermarket, food is more plentiful than it is, say, in

Moscow. But a German economy, any German economy, must be in deep trouble if it cannot make even bottles of sauerkraut look attractive. But what lightens everything in a lovely, astonishing fashion are the chattering crowds of East Berliners at the crossing points, waiting to leave as if it were the most natural thing in the world. Most are going for the day, complete with bags, babies, and beaming smiles, heading for the bright lights of West Berlin.

And for citizens of a regime known for its prim moralizing, its political piety, and its claims to be untainted by the lures of Western junk, the Ossies show themselves to be endearingly human. They crowd the non-stop strip shows on Kant Strasse. The unexpected connection between vice and philosophy is a feature of West Berlin. After all, the crown (if that is the word) of Martin Luther Strasse happens to be an emporium known as Big Sexy Land. The clip joints reduced their entry fee and offered two free beers to our "Eastern guests" and reported that the crowds were "good-humored."

And so they were. They were also "different," a word that kept cropping up among West Berliners who observed the visitors closely. The Ossies manifest that special sort of raging docility that distinguishes Eastern European crowds, people accustomed to standing in line and monitoring their expectations every wish of the way. The Wessies looked upon the Ossies with a benign complexity attended by gentle satisfaction. They were, quite simply, as pleased as punch to see them in West Berlin—though not quite sure what to do with them.

And thus it was with a certain relief that the Wessies sought refuge in their bars, restaurants, and watering holes where the Ossies could not follow and sat talking excitedly over meals that only they could afford. And the Ossies would press their noses to the windows of the Paris Bar like gentle ghosts. Yet there was no discernible resentment in their stares. Ossies were to be seen striding through the most distant suburbs, stopping to stare at children playing in the park, or a man washing his car, or gathering in great crowds outside the windows of the BMW showrooms. After all, what qualitative difference is there among the objects of your fascination when you are seeing it all for the first time? It is all very natural, and not a little sad.

At the entrance to a large department store I watched a family of East Berliners, freshly arrived, wide-eyed and eerily silent. Father, mother, and a boy of about six were passing the chocolate counter. Suddenly the little boy stopped dead. He had seen the chocolates, homemade and gleaming darkly under the lights, perfection behind the glass, a costly pyramid, profligate, tempting, untouchable. His adoration passed like an electric current into his mother and father and rooted them to the spot. No one spoke. After a while, like sleepers awakening, they shook themselves and went on their way. Seeing is believing. It's not the same as having, but it will do, for a while at least.

3

The Economic Outlook
Is Bright for Berlin

Andrew J. Glass

In the context of his family's connection to Germany and
Berlin itself, Andrew J. Glass reports on the political and economic changes in Berlin since the end of World War II and
the fall of the Berlin Wall. Despite bureaucratic red tape and
high debt, Glass finds the economic outlook for Berlin to be
encouraging, especially in the high technology industry. Andrew J. Glass is senior correspondent and a columnist for Cox
Newspapers.

M y paternal grandfather, Jakob Glass, a wealthy investment banker in prewar Poland, loved to travel but dis-
dained carrying any luggage whatsoever. He embarked on
his annual grand tours of Europe without so much as a
pocket comb, having deposited in advance splendid war-
drobes and a full set of matching accessories at each of the
various luxurious hostelries where he would be stopping.

In Berlin—then, as now, an eight-hour train trip from
Warsaw—grandfather put up at the Adlon, near the Brandenburg Gate, on Unter den Linden. Well before his arrival, a hotel butler would lay out his personal cache in
cherry wood cabinets that rested on marble floors festooned
with oriental carpets. He never returned there after 1933,
when the Nazis marched through the gate to trumpet by
torchlight the advent of the Third Reich. Ten years later,
they murdered him and most of my family.

Andrew J. Glass, "Prussian Grandeur and High-Tech Gloss: Berlin Redux," *The
New Leader*, vol. 82, November 1, 1999, p. 6. Copyright © 1999 by the American
Labor Conference on International Affairs. Reproduced by permission.

Now known as the Kempenski Adlon, the hotel has recently been restored to its prewar grandeur. (A somewhat seedier embodiment, in what was then East Germany, appears in *One, Two, Three*, a 1961 movie starring the late James Cagney in the role of C.R. MacNamara, a top Coca-Cola executive.)

I strolled past the hotel a few weeks ago after visiting the newly reopened Reichstag, which once abutted the Western side of the Berlin Wall and where these days Germany's Parliament again sits in this reclaimed German capital.

Several former high Hungarian officials stood at the hotel's entrance. They were among the figures who, defying long-standing Warsaw Pact [an agreement among Communist-controlled countries during the Cold War] policies, permitted tens of thousands of East Germans who had made their way to Hungary as ostensible tourists to flee to neighboring Austria. In doing so, they created further cracks in a decrepit East German Communist regime that would soon collapse. To show his gratitude, Berlin Mayor Eberhard Diepgen had invited the Hungarians, among others, to celebrate the 10th anniversary of the Wall's demise.

Berlin has re-emerged as a bright and lively cultural metropolis. The government has already spent some $17 billion on official construction projects, including several fine museums, and is prepared to spend lots more.

Amid light beams that played off forests of cranes, Diepgen threw a big bash at the Town Hall, in the East, to mark German Unification Day. While the party was under way, neo-Nazis knocked over more than 100 gravestones at Berlin's Weissensee Jewish cemetery. I returned to my hotel, the Westin Grand on Friedrichstrasse, before the champagne corks popped.

Earlier, on the way in from Tegel Airport, the taxi driver said he had never heard of the Westin, part of an international chain that recently acquired the place as yet another dart on the board of the global economy. But he was quite familiar with the Grand, once the favorite hang-out of the Stasi, the East German secret police. Nowadays German politicians of all stripes like to stay there, because it is a short stroll from the Reichstag.

Politics in Berlin Today

Eight years ago the German Parliament voted 337 to 320 to move from Bonn, its snug postwar seat by the Rhine, back into the restored Reichstag in the heart of Berlin. British architect Norman Foster has left in place some of the Red Army's graffiti from 1945, and has added an airy dome-shaped ceiling overlooking the city that invokes the next century.

From the well of the ultramodern purple-seated chamber, German Chancellor Gerhard Schroder heads an uneasy coalition of Social Democrats and Green Party activists that has so far done little to tackle structural unemployment or rejigger a burdensome social welfare system that has retarded growth. Nor has he done much to blunt opposition within his coalition's ranks to the new Germany's precedent-breaking military involvement in Kosovo [in the former Yugoslavia]. Since Schroder's election in September 1998 ended the 16-year reign of Helmut Kohl and the Christian Democrats, the government has felt itself shunted aside by the United States as it has fallen prey to a wave of pro-Kohl nostalgia at home.

Similar sentiments were voiced to a small group of visiting American journalists in Hamburg by Helmut Schmidt, Schroder's fellow Social Democrat, who, like Kohl, remains an elder statesman of German politics. Forced from office by a Bundestag vote of no confidence in 1982, Schmidt was obliged to watch from the sidelines as Kohl masterfully presided over German reunification, bribing the longtime Communist occupiers with $60 billion (that largely went down Soviet rat holes) to get them out months ahead of the negotiated timetable.

"America has lost the certainty and predictability of the foreign policies that it enjoyed, and we enjoyed, in the past," Schmidt told us. "The American nation as a whole is not interested in foreign politics at all, and, in Congress, I find very few people with a real interest in foreign policy."

Not many in Congress would notice, yet 10 years after the Communist East Germans stood passively by as Kohl cut his deal with Moscow, unified Germany's capital remains politically divided. In the October elections to the lo-

Post–Cold War Europe

cal legislature—like Hamburg and Bremen, Berlin enjoys the status of a full German state—half the voters in the affluent western districts backed the Christian Democrats. But among the third of the city's population that lives in the east, two out of five voters chose the up and coming Party of Democratic Socialism, successor to the Communist Party that once ruled through fear.

Berlin's Social Democrats, junior partners of the Christian Democrats, fared worst of all. They blamed their poor showing on opposition to the Kosovo intervention in this traditional citadel of protest, and on the rancorous departure last March of Oskar Lafontaine, their one-time Finance Minister, party chairman and champion of sundry Leftist causes.

A Cultural Metropolis

As in the legendary era of Marlene Dietrich that followed World War I, though, Berlin has re-emerged as a bright and lively cultural metropolis. The government has already spent some $17 billion on official construction projects, including several fine museums, and is prepared to spend lots more. For every German mark in new official outlays, private developers are spending eight. Fully a tenth of the city's 1.1 million workers are directly engaged in the rebuilding process. The developers have staked out as prime real estate the wide swath of former "no man's land," a still largely barren strip where Hitler's bunker is buried and the infamous Wall stood.

But in one respect the building boom is somewhat deceptive. Berlin continues to be Germany's slowest-growing state: Its economy shrank by 0.3 per cent last year and is still shrinking. The city has lost nearly 400,000 manufacturing jobs in the past decade. Although a host of new high-tech and service industries are moving in, they have yet to take up the slack.

Federal subsidies and transfers from richer states in the west and the south currently make up only a fifth of Berlin's budget, compared with more than half prior to unification. Despite the austerity measures instituted since 1994— which helped tear into the incumbent's vote total—a tenth of the capital's $23 billion budget this year had to be financed through fresh loans, adding to a debt burden that is the highest per person of any of the country's 16 states.

Economic Optimism

Nevertheless, there is good reason for the long-term optimism one senses here. It has been said that a third of the world's construction cranes are now at work in Shanghai. If that's so, then Berlin must be running a close second in a bold bid to reflate its shaky economy and restore some of its stately Prussian grandeur—along with a fresh topping of high-tech gloss. Seen from the newly opened Reichstag dome, bright yellow cranes rise high above the scarred earth in virtually all directions, but most noticeably toward the east, where the Wall came tumbling down in November 1989. Large water-bearing steel pipes, painted in many pastel shades, line each major building site to keep it from being flooded because of Berlin's porous soil.

Unlike London or Paris, Berlin seems to have been wrenched from the sandy earth by some random force. There are no mighty rivers or harbors here, nor any natural wealth. But even if Berlin's 3.4 million residents "play in the second league," as one official here put it, Germany, the leading power today in Europe, has made a clear commitment to this city of the kind its postwar leaders never extended to Bonn.

Information age industries are vibrant and growing in a post–Cold War Europe that the Nazis could never have imagined, even in their wildest 1,000-year fantasies.

Perhaps that's because, before World War II, Berlin served not only as the political seat of government but also as the core of the nation's economic, industrial and military life. When a divided land rose from the ruins of World War II, the Western part opted for a decentralized, federated structure. Thus the powerful Bundesbank, or central bank, was placed in Frankfurt; the Federal Constitutional Court, the supreme judicial arbiter, located in Karlsruhe; and the Federal Crime Agency, the German counterpart of the FBI, was headquartered in Wiesbaden. Meantime, Hamburg emerged as the center for many national news outlets, and vital national cultural institutions blossomed in such cities as Munich, the Bavarian capital, and Dusseldorf.

Soon most everything, save the German Defense Ministry—still a sensitive issue for the Russians and some other Europeans—will come together again in Berlin. But the rapidly paced consolidation has run into some snags. Washington is in a stew over Berlin's refusal to shift two streets near the Brandenburg Gate roughly 100 feet. Otherwise, says U.S. Ambassador John Kornblum, security concerns will make it impossible to build a new embassy in the open field near the bulldozed Wall, where it stood in 1941. Kornblum adds: "The overall German view of things is, 'We have a way of life here. We would like to find a way to deal with the hi-tech revolution and still preserve that way of life.'"

The Growth of High-Tech Business

Information age industries are vibrant and growing in a post–Cold War Europe that the Nazis could never have imagined, even in their wildest 1,000-year fantasies. Entrepreneurs find themselves hampered, however, by habits and work rules ingrained in a social system (at least in Germany) essentially put into place by [German chancellor] Otto von Bismarck over a century ago.

One example is the predicament of Siemens AG, whose sprawling Berlin complex was flattened by Allied bombers and Soviet artillery. Today it is a global electronics power-house, ranking behind General Electric and IBM in overall revenues. The high-tech sector of the new pan-European economy, led by Siemens (and Finland's Nokia), is showing clear signs of being ready to compete with, and in some cases surpass, its U.S. rivals. But the surge in the 15-nation European Union (EU) is being held back by excessive reg-ulation, chronic high unemployment and the reluctance to abandon outdated business practices.

Siemens executives have so aggressively courted cus-tomers abroad, that 70 per cent of the company's business is international. Its stock has doubled in value during the last year. "After 152 years in business, we're in the process of drastically changing our corporate culture," Karl-Hermann Baumann, chairman of Siemens powerful supervisory board, told us during a visit to Munich, where the company began anew after losing its Berlin assets. "We're becoming a lot less bureaucratic and a lot more entrepreneurial. And we're focusing our core business increasingly on informa-tion and communications technology."

Often powered by Siemens switches, the Continent's 320 million people are fast being wired up for the next mil-lennium. Nearly a dozen firms are laying fiber optic net-works through Germany to link the Atlantic to the Urals, offering a broad communications backbone for the Internet. These new neural networks have already had a definite im-pact on the European market. The cost of a 10-year lease on a jumbo 155-megabit data circuit between Paris and Berlin has fallen from $12 million two years ago to $2 million.

The competitive wave has led, in turn, to declining long-distance charges. In Germany, they have fallen to less than 10 cents a minute, comparable to the prevailing rates in the United States. Wired customers are increasingly using price rankings posted on the Internet to find the best deal. And digital TV sets in German hotel rooms offer keyboard-enabled Internet access, albeit with a fast meter running.

Notwithstanding the advantages of a single market—

and, for 11 EU [European Union] members, a single currency—e-commerce across European frontiers lags well behind the frantic U.S. pace. In part this is because most European telecommunications firms charge their customers by the minute, thereby cutting incentives for leisurely Internet trolling.

"It's all starting to come together," said Baumann, the Siemens chairman, as he stowed his tiny company-made phone and invited his guests to lunch. "And one reason it's working is because we're offering our people lifetime employability [i.e. training] instead of lifetime employment."

A New World

Berlin is of course quite a different place—lodged smack in the midst of quite a different Europe—than the one that existed at the end of World War II. At that time my father, having escaped the Holocaust, vowed he would never again return to either Germany or Poland. Over the ensuing years he often roamed the world, yet he kept the pledge until his death in 1993.

My son has yet to visit Poland either. But while still in college he did spend a summer studying at Heidelberg University.

In going to Germany, Sam broke with the lordly travel pattern of his great-grandfather, Jakob, and checked his bag at the economy counter. But he has followed in Jakob's footsteps by recently beginning an investment banking career. If his new Manhattan employers like his work, perhaps someday they will dispatch him to Berlin. Maybe they will even put him up, for $250 a night, at his Polish ancestor's favorite hotel, near the stone arch through which Nazi storm troopers marched to the East and German freedom seekers bolted to the West.

4

Economic and Social Difficulties Plague Berlin

Belinda Cooper

In the following article, Belinda Cooper summarizes the social, political, and economic histories of Berlin, acknowledging that the Berlin of today is a natural extension of these historical patterns.

In social encounters between East and West, she finds that a division still exists, primarily characterized by West German disdain of the East and East German defiance toward Westerners. Politically, left-leaning Socialist and Communist parties still maintain some influence, capitalizing on East German resentment of the West. In addition, a large influx of foreign immigrants has added to a xenophobic atmosphere that has created further divisions. Lastly, the Berlin economy is struggling, largely as a result of profit taking immediately following the fall of the wall and the loss of its industrial base. Despite the "crisis mentality" of the city, Cooper believes that Berlin may rise above its problems and serve an important role in the European community. Belinda Cooper is a senior fellow at the World Policy Institute, a research and education policy center that seeks solutions to critical problems facing the United States and the world.

It has not been easy for residents of the eastern section of Berlin since 1989. With the fall of the Berlin Wall and unification a year later, their city began to be transformed around them, often without their consent or participation. First it was the products in the stores; almost overnight,

Belinda Cooper, "The Changing Face of Berlin," *World Policy Journal*, vol. 15, Fall 1998, pp. 57–68. Copyright © 1998 by *World Policy Journal*. Reproduced by permission.

brightly colored junk food, dozens of different brands, and an array of flavors and choices replaced the simple but serviceable butter, milk, and washing soap of the East German shops. Then it was the place names—streets and subway stops named for socialists, communists, and resistance fighters either reverted to their old Prussian names or were given new ones. The statues, too, the Marxes, Engelses, and Lenins, slowly disappeared, to be replaced by concrete-and-glass shopping centers. Their money, their laws, then their jobs—all were swept away on the tide of change.

It is in Berlin, the formerly divided city where East and West confront one another every day, that the dramas of German unification are played out most intensely.

But when Berlin's government began to phase out the green and red men representing "Walk" and "Don't Walk" on East Berlin's traffic lights, ostensibly because of a European Union uniformity requirement, that was going too far. In no time, East Berliners, as though projecting years of frustration onto the small figures, had turned the determined-looking green man in a hat who stood for "Walk" (along with his more stolid red brother) into a symbol of East German identity. The little men soon graced products from T-shirts to mouse pads to keychains, proving that the East had quietly been learning from the West all along, at least where marketing was concerned. There was even a website, filled with pictures, background information, and poems dedicated to the green and red figures. The organizers of the campaign, a group of mainly East Berliners calling themselves the "Committee to Save the Ampelmannchen," were themselves caught by surprise at the speed with which their idea caught on. In the end, for almost the first time since 1990, the East won; the little men stayed.

Of course, this was a fight with few political implications, threatening nothing more than the compulsive West German (and now arguably European) desire for uniformity—a need that, in any case, is rarely as strong in Berlin as elsewhere. Conservatives who had earlier fought successfully to change street names honoring communist resistance figures would have had much more difficulty arguing the necessity of substituting the West's slender, rather boring Walk/Don't Walk men for the East's chubbier green and red Ampelmannchen. And in a city that has been on the verge of bankruptcy since federal subsidies were cut off in 1994, changing "Don't Walk" signs would have looked frivolous. But despite the playfulness of the campaign, the intensity with which Easterners embraced "their" trafficlight men reflected the tensions—between East and West, between change and tradition—that continue to shape the city nearly nine years after the fall of the Berlin Wall.

Friction between East and West, and worries about change, have grown throughout Germany since 1989, but it is in Berlin, the formerly divided city where East and West confront one another every day, that the dramas of German unification are played out most intensely. Only in Berlin did a Western administration assume control of an East German city overnight, and only there have West Germans undergone almost as many transformations in their lives as East Germans. As Berlin gears up to be capital of Europe's most powerful country, in fact as well as in name (most government offices are slated to be moved there by the year 1999), change and the responses to it have become part of the city's fundamental experience.

A Cultural Capital

Berlin, for centuries a seat of Prussian nobility, became Germany's capital in 1871, but the culturally vibrant, decadent metropolis its name generally conjures up is the Berlin of the early decades of the twentieth century.

Particularly in the 1920s, in the tumultuous years following the First World War, Berlin became Germany's, and Europe's, center of cultural and political ferment. Artists, writers, and intellectuals faced off, first against authoritarian rulers and then, in the Weimar Republic, against the fascists, as freedom and lively experimentation flourished in defiance of Prussian order and bureaucracy.

The rise of Nazism brought an end to this brilliant but brief epoch in Berlin's history; the city's artists, intellectuals, and politicians were murdered or went into exile, and during the Second World War much of Berlin was bombed into rubble. After the war, the city, perched on the cusp of two warring systems, was divided, first politically, then physically, by the Berlin Wall. Though neither part of Berlin would regain the glitter of the prewar years, both half-cities retained a reputation for openness that went beyond their official status as showcases for their respective systems. East Berlin, with its proximity to the West, was a magnet for young people and dissidents. West Berlin attracted young draft resisters (Berlin's occupied status meant draft laws did not apply there) and people looking for an alternative to the bland materialism of postwar West Germany. In this way, even in division, Berlin continued to discomfit those in power, though within the circumscribed confines of the Cold War.

Since the fall of the Wall, change has buffeted Berlin from all sides, embracing all levels of society. In its politics, its economy, its social relationships, Berlin is a city in transition, reevaluating itself even as it endeavors to retain its fundamental character. Berliners are very much aware of their history; in part for that very reason, Berlin will not again be the tempestuous, strife-torn metropolis of the 1920s, any more than it will become the imperial capital Hitler envisioned. Its role in a developing, unified Europe is likely to be less turbulent. In the new century, this role may well be determined by Berlin's ability to resolve its underlying tensions—between East and West, immigrants and natives, the authority of the federal government and the skepticism of Berlin's citizens—in constructive fashion.

Berliner Disaffection

After the fall of the Berlin Wall, even the most liberal West Berliners became cultural chauvinists, seeing nothing worthwhile in the experiences of East Germans and often projecting their own worst qualities onto the Easterners. Accustomed to living well in the subsidized West Berlin economy, they nevertheless resented the consumerist tendencies of the product-starved East Germans crowding their local stores. Many West Berliners were disturbed by the disappearance of their safe "island" when the wall that had provided protection as well as isolation came down. Others had more serious concerns. Berlin was a center of the struggles of the 1960s, when young Germans rebelled against the entrenched structural and human holdovers of the Nazi system, as well as against the values of that generation. Veterans of the struggle feared that what they saw as undemocratic, authoritarian, Prussian influences from East

Germany would nullify the gains in democratic consciousness made by their generation. Few recognized, or saw any
role for, the resourcefulness, independence, and even
courage many East Germans had developed to cope with
life in a totalitarian society.

---

*In its politics, its economy, its social relationships,
Berlin is a city in transition, reevaluating itself
even as it endeavors to retain its fundamental
character.*

Former West German chancellor Willy Brandt's famous
prediction, as the Berlin Wall fell, that "what belongs together will now grow together" was taken by most West
Germans to mean East Germans would become just like
them, and at the time, few East Germans had the confidence
or the desire to insist on a separate identity. But over time,
Germans on both sides of the former divide—like North-
erners and Southerners after the American Civil War—have
slowly come to realize that years of divergent experience
have indeed created a separate East German "identity" that
is not going to disappear quickly.

More recently, though, the East-West issue has receded
from the top of Berlin's agenda. The disdain shown by West
Berliners toward East Berliners and the resentful defiance
of East Berliners that superseded the mutual curiosity of the
first post-Wall months have themselves become more ritual
than reality. East and West Berliners have long since disengaged and gone their separate ways. Voluntary mingling—
even visits to the other side of the city—is rare. . . .

But the East-West divide, and the discrimination
against the East that accompanies it, are more than just psy-
chological phenomena. Until recently, civil servants from
East Berlin working side by side in offices with Western colleagues received less pay, regardless of ability. Moreover, the
ranks of Eastern civil servants were slashed after unification;
their training was considered to be inferior, or they were
tainted by a history of collaboration with the East German
secret police. In their place, West German and West Berlin
bureaucrats began flooding East Berlin's schools and offices,
taking over top posts they might not have been able to

achieve in the West and earning more than their Eastern compatriots, while more competent East Berliners were pushed into the lower echelons. Now, although pay has been equalized for all "Beamten"—Germany's thoroughly coddled, highly compensated, unfireable tenured public servants, who include teachers, government administrators, firefighters, police officers, museum workers, and anyone in any way connected with Germany's vast state apparatus— there continue to be fewer tenured civil servants in the East, so that East Berliners tend to be found in the lower-ranking, lower-paying jobs.

Pay differentials are not confined to public-sector jobs. An editor at a Berlin daily located in the East, which targets an Eastern audience and has many Eastern employees, told me not long ago that the West German media conglomerate that runs the paper pays all Eastern employees, regardless of position, less than their Western colleagues. After criticizing this state of affairs, he launched into a tirade about the East German lack of understanding of democracy. This quite common West German view of a backward Eastern political consciousness has only been strengthened by the strong rightwing showing in state elections earlier this year in the eastern state of Saxony-Anhalt.

The Politics of Berlin

But given their situation, it is not surprising that East Berliners, like East Germans in general, are feeling disaffected, and this is changing the political contours of the city. In the 1995 city elections, the top party in East Berlin was the Party of Democratic Socialism, or PDS, the reformed successor to East Germany's Communist Party, and left-leaning parties in general (the PDS, the Social Democrats, and the Greens) far outstripped the conservative Christian Democrats (CDU). The former Communists have almost no support in West Berlin, where the CDU retains a slight majority. The mayor is a Christian Democrat, and the city is governed by a Christian Democratic–Social Democratic coalition. But because of its consistent strength in the East, the PDS now colors Berlin politics.

West Germans have wondered at the PDS's staying power since the early days of unification. The majority of the party's small membership is made up of old party cadres, who display a typically communist mixture of radical politics and conservative behavior. But another faction of the membership is quite young and truly radical, and elements of the party's program mirror the programs of the Greens and Social Democrats. The party's voters include both young and old, and people with varying income levels, although the party admittedly does best in the areas of Berlin most heavily settled by former Communist Party members and secret police employees. The reasons for the PDS's success are not difficult to discern. The party has capitalized on the resentment engendered by the West's treatment of East Germany, and has tapped into Easterners' defiant response to the redbaiting of the established Western parties, with its implicitly anti–East German rhetoric. Also, the PDS has proven itself capable of cooperative governing on the local level, an important aspect of Berlin politics that has earned it grudging respect. . . .

Overall, Berlin has become a more leftleaning city as a result of unification. This will not necessarily lead, however, to leftleaning governments like the short-lived Social Democratic–Green coalition of the late 1980s that ended with the fall of the Wall. All parties in Berlin categorically refuse to share power in a coalition with the PDS, despite its numbers in the eastern half of the city. Though they cooperate locally, on a citywide level the taint of communism—even former communism—is anathema. Ultimately, though, it is quite possible that, given the CDU's weakness in East Berlin, the arrival of the federal government with its attendant disruptions, and the likely victory of the Social Democrats in national elections this year, Berlin's government will move to the left in the 1999 municipal elections. Such a leftward tilt would in turn influence the city's relationship with the federal government soon to be in its midst—especially since the PDS is the strongest party in the Mitte district, where the government will be based.

Not an Economic Mecca

On March 2, 1998, Delta Airlines flew from New York direct to Berlin for the last time. Delta now offers a direct flight to Warsaw instead, skipping Berlin in favor of a true Eastern boom town. Tourists still visit Berlin, but business travelers are scarce. Berlin has not lived up to the promise, or the illusions, of the early post-Wall years. Economically, the city—suffering from lower productivity and higher unemployment than most of Germany—is playing a waiting game, hoping that the arrival of the federal government in 1999 will pick up its floundering economy. . . .

East and West Berliners have long since disengaged and gone their separate ways. Voluntary mingling—even visits to the other side of the city—is rare.

It was not unification per se that played havoc with the city's economy. In the years following the fall of the Wall, Berlin's governments consistently failed to face the consequences of the loss of the city's special status. A gold rush mentality prevailed, coupled with an exaggerated sense of Berlin's future prospects and the lingering confidence that Bonn would make up any deficits. West German and West Berlin businesses scrambled to make money in the East. Investors were granted huge tax writeoffs to build in most of Berlin. Buildings popped up like mushrooms in every empty space; East German buildings that were in the way were simply torn down. Often the new construction was slapdash and at least as ugly as the Communist-era architecture it replaced. Friedrichstrasse, which had been a busy shopping street before the Wall went up and then languished for 40 years, now boasts a row of not particularly attractive, super-modern glass-and-concrete edifices built by famous architects and filled with stores selling goods too expensive for the average East Berliner. As common as the new stores, however, are the "for rent" signs draped across empty office buildings throughout the city. According to the magazine *Der Spiegel*, Berlin now boasts 1.3 million square meters of empty office space. At the same time, as people return to Western Germany or move to the countryside, Berlin's population, which rose somewhat after the fall of the Wall, has been gradually dropping, to just over 3.4 million today. (The city's population was nearly 4.5 million in 1939; by the end of the Second World War, it stood at 3 million.)

Meanwhile, Berlin's industrial base has been lost as East Berlin industries have been closed down—in part because of inefficiency, but also because of targeted efforts by Western businesses to eliminate possible East German competitors.

Western businesses, too, having lost the investment subsidies and tax breaks that had made Berlin attractive, moved out of the city to the neighboring state of Brandenburg or elsewhere entirely. Nor did the battles to win over the East Berlin consumer promote capitalist competition: after years in which supermarkets in the East seemed to change Western owners almost monthly, for example, one large West German grocery chain now dominates East Berlin.

Berlin has not lived up to the promise, or the illusions, of the early post-Wall years.

Berlin's economic disorder also derives from the corruption and patronage politics that grew up as a result of the city's postwar isolation. Berlin journalist Mathew Rose made waves in 1997 with a detailed expose of the workings of Berlin's entrenched system of cronyism, in which politicians responsible for distributing the subsidies that poured in so liberally from Bonn sat on the boards of many of the organizations, including state-run banks, sports clubs, and corporations, that benefited from their largesse. Rose revealed that politicians went so far as to pay off journalists and control media outlets to ensure that pet projects came to fruition. A notorious example was Berlin's 1993 application to host the Year 2000 Olympics, a massive and ultimately unsuccessful public relations project—opposed by a majority of Berliners—that cost the city tens of millions of dollars, while putting several millions in the pockets of companies that participated in the public relations effort. Tellingly, several of the major actors in that fiasco now hold important positions throughout the city—even in the quasigovernmental organization that is now promoting investment in Berlin. Still, Berlin's Social Democratic commissioner for finances, Annette Fugmann-Heesing, who was brought in from West Germany in the hope of clearing away some of the ingrown political thickets, appears to have made some progress in creating a modicum of transparency in the city's murky finances.

The Change to a Service Economy

Berlin now hopes to develop a servicebased economy, but at present there is no one to serve: Germany's financial center is in Frankfurt, its media center in Hamburg, its cultural centers in Munich and Cologne, and its trade fairs in Hanover and Leipzig. Still, the significance of the new service focus should not be underestimated in a city (in fact, an entire country) in which, until recently, the word had little meaning. Berlin salespeople traditionally took insult if customers interrupted their telephone conversations, let alone requested help, and shopkeepers, waiters, clerks, and other service personnel were notoriously rude. Stores closed punctually at 6:00 P.M., prohibited by federal law from staying open later; closing was also mandated on Sundays and Saturday afternoons. Though Westerners like to complain about East German service, the problem was endemic to both parts of the city (in fact, stores in East Berlin were likely to keep later hours).

This has changed visibly over the last few years; Berliners are telling stories of polite service these days, with astonished pleasure, the way New Yorkers speak of the drop in crime. An extension of this, at last, was the national change in store closing hours "a bigger step forward than the fall of the Wall," as one American expatriate recently termed it, with only slight exaggeration. In 1996, as unions and small business associations fought a frantic, misguided rearguard action, the federal government decided to allow stores to stay open as late as 8:00 P.M. during the week and 4:00 P.M. on Saturday; some small shops now even open on Sunday. The tension that used to descend upon the city right before the stores closed has visibly waned, the stress on working mothers, in particular, has lessened, and shopping streets that were once dead in the evening have livened up. . . .

Insecurities

Despite such improvements, Berliners are doing more worrying than usual—which is saying a lot in a country where people tend to dwell on the negative. Even with all the city's problems, Berliners, like Germans in general, still enjoy a high standard of living by American standards. But Berliners, West and East, fear a creeping Americanization of Germany—the end of the welfare state and the cold, hard climate of competition.

The fear is unfounded; Germany is not the United States, and a commitment to social responsibility exists across the political spectrum. Even a cursory examination of the system of social benefits and entitlements reveals that the German government could cut benefits for years without beginning to approach American levels. A recent rise in the sliding-scale fees for state-subsidized day-care in Berlin, for example, resulted in a top fee of less than $300 a month for families earning over about $70,000.

Still, after years when only East Berliners felt the harsh reality of cuts and change (and were often dismissed as ungrateful whiners when they complained), the reduction in federal subsidies has recently begun to make itself felt in the western half of the city, spreading East German insecurities to the West. With the arrival of Finance Commissioner Fugmann-Heesing two years ago, budget cuts became the order of the day. Public transportation became more expensive, cultural subsidies fell, and public facilities, such as swimming pools, raised their rates. The budgets of Berlin's three major universities were slashed, leading to widespread protests. True, students are not yet required to pay tuition, cultural activities are still widely available and affordable, and workers continue to enjoy six weeks of vacation a year and to receive a month's salary as a Christmas bonus. Where the cuts have had an effect—for example, in subsidies to theaters and museums—they have encouraged some creative thinking in a cultural landscape that often seems stiflingly dependent on handouts. But they have also increased the overall sense of unease among Berliners. They have also had the salutary effect of bringing together West and East in shared indignation. Cuts in the education budget and proposed changes to the free university system, for example, recently united university students from both sides of the city in a campaign to save their universities, and East Berliners played an important role in the protests. Solidarity in opposition to cutbacks in welfare state entitlements is one way the two halves of the city may yet overcome some of their divisions.

Building New Walls

For 40 years, West Berlin, like the East Germany in which it was situated, was isolated (though of course to a different degree) from the realities of Europe. With the fall of the Wall, Berlin became a more open city than it had been in years. Its newly porous borders meant an influx of foreigners: East Europeans, ethnic Germans, and asylum-seekers from many countries flowed in, adding another element to the East German West German equation. In 1990, for example, Romanian Gypsies descended upon Berlin, confronting residents with the completely unfamiliar spectacle of poverty and begging on West Berlin's poshest streets. Germany acted quickly to stem the tide, erecting a new "wall" of visa requirements, and these legal moves were tracked by popular violence against foreigners in both West and East Germany.

Chancellor Helmut Kohl responded to right-wing demands by tightening Germany's relatively generous asylum laws, but the reduction in asylum-seekers failed to have the promised effect of lessening xenophobic and racist violence. According to social workers, in fact, right-wing youngsters saw the government's response as a vindication of their views. Of course, foreigners are not the problem, but merely the scapegoat: the anti-foreigner and right-wing extremist sentiment among east German young people, in particular, is attributed by observers to the uncertainty of life in the East since unification, to the dismantling of East Germany's broad infrastructure of youth organizations and clubs, and to the economic dislocations and lack of confidence in the future experienced by this population.

Even with all the city's problems, Berliners, like Germans in general, still enjoy a high standard of living by American standards.

Berlin has had its share of neo-Nazi attacks on foreigners and people considered to be different, though such attacks have occurred less frequently there than in other parts of Germany. In fact, the violence and the government's problematic legal response to it brought millions into Berlin's streets in the early 1990s for demonstrations of solidarity with foreigners. But the city's meld of East and West makes its situation more complex than elsewhere in Germany. . . .

Berlin remains culturally diverse nevertheless. Some 13 percent of the population holds a foreign passport; the Russian and Polish communities have grown exponentially since 1989, and the Jewish community has exploded, as Russian Jews flock to the city. Yugoslavian refugees and East Berlin's Vietnamese guest workers, or at least those permitted to remain after unification, have added to the mix.

Though the more open borders have also brought the East European mafia and greater crime, Berliners tend to be proud of their city's tolerant tradition and are not prone, at least publicly, to blaming their problems on foreigners. The police department has even introduced ethnic sensitivity training and recruited members of minority groups. But the difficulties faced by the Turkish population, coupled with the rise in xenophobia throughout the country and Germany's continued resistance to the concept of official and regulated immigration, make the issue of multiculturalism a volatile one even in cosmopolitan Berlin. . . .

Berlin United

There's no doubt that life has gotten more difficult in Berlin, now that the protected, subsidized life of the walled city is gone for both sides. People feel more exposed, and in some ways they are. The outside world has intruded upon Berlin, even more so than upon the rest of Germany. Change has brought a sense of dislocation, first to the East, and now also to the West. Tensions between West and East add to the mix.

Where the story in the early years was all about the West's influence on the East, for good or evil, and about the East's resistance or acquiescence to it, the picture was never as simple as that. Now East Berliners have asserted themselves politically on a broad scale, and they are also slowly gaining influence on more subtle levels, through everyday involvement in the city's social, cultural, and economic life. Many East Germans developed their own means of showing independence and expressing creativity, especially in the old regime's last years. They learned out of necessity how to circumvent rigid bureaucratic, political, economic, and social structures, a skill that will prove useful as Germany reluctantly sheds some of its traditional economic practices to meet the challenges of globalization. Thus their influence is likely to become even more perceptible as time goes by.

Meanwhile, despite the crisis mentality that often pervades the city, Berlin's blend of cosmopolitan skepticism and conservative affection for tradition are keeping it on a more or less even keel. The city's tendency toward endless public debate over everything from whether and how to build a Holocaust memorial to what items to cut from the budget makes it difficult for any measure to pass without public scrutiny. Once the federal government arrives, there are sure to be perennial tussles over control of the city, and Berlin will certainly change as a result. Ultimately, though, Berlin is a difficult city to resist. Once the bureaucrats from Bonn settle in, they may find themselves adapting to Berlin as much as, if not more so than, Berlin adjusts to them.

Despite the crisis mentality that often pervades the city, Berlin's blend of cosmopolitan skepticism and conservative affection for tradition are keeping it on a more or less even keel.

Berlin's conservative side makes it easier for the city's residents to accept the fact that it is unlikely ever to regain the heights of brilliance it attained in the Weimar Republic; nor is it likely to rival New York, or even Shanghai, in economic, political, or cultural influence. The flexibility, risk-taking, and creative chaos, as well as the social inequalities, that typify today's global metropolises are more common in the former Eastern bloc, or outside Europe altogether, than they are in Germany, even in Berlin. Germany's outstanding characteristics since the war have been stability and moderation. Even today, Germans do not trust themselves with power; German institutions are purposely decentralized, and many government offices will be staying in Bonn or re-locating elsewhere, leaving Berlin only a partial capital. In a city that consisted for 40 years of two artificial constructs, the equally artificial post-1989 attempt by overzealous politicians to transform Berlin overnight into a major European center was bound in any case to fail.

But if it is allowed to develop organically, Berlin may yet play an important role in Europe. It is unique in possessing ties to both Eastern and Western Europe. East Berliners, like East Germans in general, may have complained about Russian domination (though less so than East Europeans with a longer history of subservience to Russia), but they learned Russian, spent their vacations in Hungary and Romania, and interacted professionally with East European colleagues. And Berlin has attracted large populations of East European immigrants. If East and West Berliners succeed in overcoming the rift that continues to separate them, and if West Berliners learn to respect and utilize the knowledge and experience of their Eastern compatriots, the city could play a significant role as a mediator and link between Western and Eastern Europe—a function it already performs informally.

It is of course impossible to predict where, exactly, Berlin's process of transformation will lead it. But the city's greatest strength and its greatest promise lie precisely in the interplay between the varied groups and forces that comprise it and contribute to its tensions—between its East Berliners and West Berliners, between its residents with "foreign" backgrounds and its native Germans, and between its Prussian traditions of bureaucracy and authority and its ordinary citizens' skepticism and tradition of protest. With luck, this interplay will turn Berlin into a capital city worthy of Europe's strongest power—and one that will keep it from complacency.

Chronology

May 8, 1945
World War II ends. Germany and Berlin are divided into separate sectors controlled by the United States, Great Britain, France, and the Soviet Union (USSR).

June 5, 1947
George C. Marshall, U.S. secretary of state, outlines a European aid program to be known as the Marshall Plan.

June 24, 1948
Soviet forces blockade West Berlin. Western Allies stage the Berlin Airlift to supply the people of West Berlin.

April 4, 1949
The North Atlantic Treaty Organization (NATO) is formed.

May 12, 1949
The Soviet blockade of Berlin is lifted.

Summer 1952
The border between East and West Germany is closed.

1953
Nikita S. Khrushchev becomes the leader of the USSR.

June 17, 1953
East Berliners riot in the streets to protest failed government policies. The Soviets respond with military might and crush the revolt.

May 14, 1955
The Warsaw Pact is signed by the Soviet Union, Poland, Czechoslovakia, Hungary, Romania, Bulgaria, and Albania to ensure a unified Socialist bloc to counter NATO.

November 27, 1958
Khrushchev issues an ultimatum to the Western allies that they must leave West Berlin within six months.

1961
John F. Kennedy becomes the thirty-fifth president of the United States.

April 1961
President Kennedy fails in an attempt to oust socialist dictator Fidel Castro from the leadership of Cuba.

August 13, 1961
East Germans build a wall separating East and West Berlin.

June 1963
President Kennedy delivers his famous "I Am a Berliner" speech at the Berlin Wall, pledging to protect West Berlin's citizens from any act of aggression.

October 1965
President Kennedy orders a naval blockade of Cuba to prevent Soviet shipments of nuclear missiles. The tense standoff is known as the Cuban Missile Crisis. After thirteen days, the Soviets back down and remove all missiles from Cuba.

1971
Erich Honecker takes over as leader of East Germany from Walter Ulbricht, maintaining a hard-line policy against those attempting to cross the Berlin Wall.

1974
The United States establishes relations with East Germany.

June 12, 1987
President Ronald Reagan's famous "Tear Down This Wall" speech is delivered at the Brandenburg Gate in West Berlin, Germany.

September 10, 1989
Hungary opens its border to East German refugees.

September–October 1989
Egon Krenz replaces Erich Honecker as the Communist leader in East Berlin because of pro-democracy demonstrations in the city.

November 4, 1989
The East German government resigns in the face of anti-Communist demonstrations in East Berlin.

November 9, 1989
The Berlin Wall comes down.

October 3, 1990
Germany is officially reunited.

For Further Research

Books

Michael R. Beschloss, *The Crisis Years: Kennedy and Khrushchev, 1960–1963.* New York: Edward Burlingame, 1991.

Curtis Cate, *The Ides of August: The Berlin Wall Crisis, 1961.* New York: M. Evans, 1978.

Honoré M. Catudal, *Kennedy and the Berlin Wall Crisis: A Case Study in U.S. Decision Making.* Berlin: Berlin-Verlag, 1980.

Eleanor Lansing Dulles, *Berlin: The Wall Is Not Forever.* Chapel Hill: University of North Carolina Press, 1967.

Doris M. Epler, *The Berlin Wall: How It Rose and Why It Fell.* Brookfield, CT: Millbrook, 1992.

John Lewis Gaddis, *We Now Know: Rethinking Cold War History.* New York: Oxford University Press, 1997.

Pierre Galante with Jack Miller, *The Berlin Wall.* New York: Doubleday, 1965.

Norman Gelb, *The Berlin Wall.* London: M. Joseph, 1986.

Willard A. Heaps, *The Wall of Shame.* New York: Duell, Sloan & Pearce, 1964.

Deane and David Heller, *The Berlin Wall.* London: Frederick Muller, 1962.

Tom Heneghan, *Unchained Eagle: Germany After the Wall.* London: Pearson Education, 2000.

Christopher Hilton, *The Wall: The People's Story.* Stroud, UK: Sutton, 2001.

John W. Keller, *Germany, the Wall and Berlin: Internal Politics During an International Crisis.* New York: Vantage, 1964.

Steven Kelman, *Behind the Berlin Wall: An Encounter in East Germany.* Boston: Houghton Mifflin, 1972.

Anthony Kemp, *Escape from Berlin.* London: Boxtree, 1987.

Giles MacDonogh, *Berlin: A Portrait of Its History, Politics, Architecture, and Society.* New York: St. Martin's, 1998.

John Mander, *Berlin: Hostage for the West.* London: Penguin, 1962.

A. James McAdams, *East Germany and Détente: Building Authority After the Wall.* New York: Cambridge University Press, 1985.

Richard L. Merritt and Anna J. Merritt, eds., *Living with the Wall: West Berlin, 1961–1985.* Durham, NC: Duke University Press, 1985.

Eric Morris, *Blockade: Berlin and the Cold War.* London: Hamish Hamilton, 1973.

Jack M. Schick, *The Berlin Crisis, 1958–1962.* Philadelphia: University of Pennsylvania Press, 1971.

Ernst Schürer, Manfred Keune, and Philip Jenkins, eds., *The Berlin Wall: Representations and Perspectives.* New York: P. Lang, 1996.

Peter Schweizer, ed., *The Fall of the Berlin Wall: Reassessing the Causes and Consequences of the End of the Cold War.* Washington, DC: William J. Casey Institute of the Center for Security Policy, 2000.

Robert Slusser, *The Berlin Crisis of 1961: Soviet-American Relations and the Struggle for Power in the Kremlin, June–November 1961.* Baltimore: Johns Hopkins University Press, 1973.

Terry Tillman, *The Writings on the Wall: Peace at the Berlin Wall.* Santa Monica, CA: Twenty-Two Sevenths, 1990.

Ann Tusa, *The Last Division: A History of Berlin, 1945–1989.* Reading, MA: Addison-Wesley, 1997.

Marie Ueda, *Testimony of the Twentieth Century: Before and After the Berlin Wall.* San Francisco: M.I. Productions, 1996.

Andreas Wenger, *Living with Peril: Eisenhower, Kennedy, and Nuclear Weapons.* Lanham, MD: Rowman & Littlefield, 1997.

David Wetzel, ed., *From the Berlin Museum to the Berlin Wall: Essays on the Cultural and Political History of Modern Germany.* Westport, CT: Praeger, 1996.

Peter Wyden, *Wall: The Inside Story of Divided Berlin.* New York: Simon and Schuster, 1989.

Vladislav Zubok and Constantine Pleshakov, *Inside the Kremlin's Cold War: From Stalin to Khrushchev.* Cambridge, MA: Harvard University Press, 1996.

Periodicals

Arnold Beichman, "Reagan's Legacy: How the Cold War Was Won," *Washington Times*, November 5, 1999.

Helle Bering, "After the Berlin Wall: More Freedom Ten Years Later," *Washington Times*, November 3, 1999.

Stephen Brockmann, "Living Where the Wall Was: What Still Divides the Germans," *Commonweal*, September 24, 1993.

Pete Du Pont, "Eastern Europe: Cold War's End Doesn't Mean West Should Be Inactive," *Dallas Morning News*, May 27, 1996.

Nathan Gardels, "Gorbachev: Ten Years After Fall of the Wall, NATO Runs the World," *Global Viewpoint*, November 4, 1999.

R.L. Garthoff, "Berlin 1961: The Record Corrected," *Foreign Policy*, Fall 1991.

Mikhail Gorbachev, "'Doomed to Disappear': The Reformer on the Last Days of the Wall—and Why Communism Crumbled," *Newsweek*, November 8, 1999.

Hope M. Harrison, "Conflict in Soviet Bloc Created Berlin Wall, Not the Cold War," *Morning Call*, August 13, 1996.

Jim Hoagland, "'Popular Capitalism' a Pathway for Europe," *Seattle Post-Intelligencer*, November 28, 1999.

Robert Jensen, "Ten Years After the Berlin Wall Fell, It's Time to Junk the War Machine," *Austin American-Statesman*, November 6, 1999.

J.W. Kimball, "Columnist Overrates Reagan's Contributions to the Cold War," *Washington Times*, November 15, 1999.

Sabine, Kleinert, "Ten Years On—the Invisible Berlin Wall Remains," *Lancet*, November 13, 1999.

Charles Krauthammer, "Mixed Feelings About End of Cold War," *Buffalo News*, November 16, 1999.

A. James McAdams, "An Obituary for the Berlin Wall," *World Policy Journal*, Spring 1990.

Gunter Minnerup, "Opening Up a New Europe? (German Unification and Changes in Eastern Europe)," *Nation*, December 4, 1989.

Martin Peretz, "The Gorbachev Tease: Haven't We Seen This Act Before?" *New Republic*, July 10, 1989.

Edelbert Richter, "Ten Years After the Fall—Germany: The Disappointments of . . ." *Transitions*, January 1999.

John Rodden, "The Berlin Wall Lives: Today It's a Mental Construct," *Commonweal*, September 22, 2000.

Daniel Schorr, "Gorbachev's Doctrine," *New Leader*, November 13, 1989.

———, "Television and the Wall," *New Leader*, November 1, 1999.

Jamieson Spencer, "The Good That Socialism Wrought," *St. Louis Post-Dispatch*, March 24, 1997.

Caspar W. Weinberger, "Ten Years On and the Lessons of Victory," *Forbes*, August 23, 1999.

Rosemary Yardley, "Berlin Is Still a City Divided, but by a Mental Wall," *News and Record*, July 24, 1996.

Websites

The Berlin Wall, http://userpage.chemie.fu-berlins.de/BIW/wall.html. Maintained by Burkhard Kirste, a professor at a Berlin university, this site provides a brief history of the Berlin Wall along with links to photograph galleries, art galleries, and essays about the wall.

Berlin Wall Online, www.dailysoft.com/berlinwall. This website chronicles the history of the Berlin Wall, including an archive of photographs and texts. A list of frequently asked questions, a time line, art galleries, and links to other sites are also present. Photographer Heiko Burkhardt maintains this site and includes his own photographs of Berlin Wall graffiti.

Berlin Wall Ten Years After, www.time.com/time/daily/special/berlin/index.html. Offered by the publishers of *Time* magazine, this website details, through essays and an extensive photographic gallery, the conditions of life in

Berlin before and after the fall of the wall. A time line and biographies of important figures are also presented.

Building the Berlin Wall, www.bbc.co.uk/worldservice/ people/highlights/010815_berlinwalls.html. This website, presented by the BBC World Service, outlines a brief history of the building of the Berlin Wall with links to related stories, histories, facts, and time lines.

Chronik der Wende—The Fall of the Berlin Wall, www. chronikderwende.de/english/overview.jsp. A detailed time line of events in the months leading up to the fall of the Berlin Wall are documented in this website presented by ORB (Ostdeutscher Rundfunk Brandenburg), the East German Broadcasting Corporation. Brief biographies of important leaders are highlighted.

The Cold War, www.cnn.com/SPECIALS/cold.war/ episodes/09/. Presented by CNN, this website examines the role of the Berlin Wall as part of Cold War history. A brief history of the wall is supplemented with personal biographies of important persons, historical documents, photographs, maps, and radio broadcasts.

A Concrete Curtain: The Life and Death of the Berlin Wall, www.wall-berlin.org/gb/berlin.htm. This exhibit details the beginning of the Cold War, the 1958 crisis, the phases of the wall's construction, the important events of life in Berlin during the wall's presence, the fall of the wall, and the wall as it stands today. Each section is supplemented with photographs, and the site includes maps, significant quotations, a time line, and a bibliography. The website's curator is Cyril Buffet, a historian based in Paris.

German Propaganda Archive, www.calvin.edu/academic/ cas/gpa/. Maintained by Calvin College in Grand Rapids, Michigan, this website offers an extensive list of full texts of German propaganda materials, both before and after the building of the Berlin Wall. Speeches by East German leaders, posters, and caricatures are also included.

Newseum, the Interactive Museum of the News: The Berlin Wall, www.newseum.org/berlinwall/index.htm. This website presents an overview of the history of the Berlin Wall, an examination of how the news differed between East and West Berlin, and a case study of Stalin's manipulation of the truth through photography. The

Newseum is supported by the Freedom Forum, a non-partisan foundation dedicated to a free press and to free speech.

Ten Years After: The Fall of Communism in East/Central Europe, www.rferl.org/nca/special/10years/index.html. Radio Free Europe/Radio Liberty presents extensive commentary on conditions after the fall of the Berlin Wall. This site also offers information on other Eastern European countries during this time period.

Index

Aarhus (Denmark), 88
Adenauer, Konrad
  German American tension and, 73
  war and, 51
Adlon (hotel), 104–105
Algeria, 52
Allied Control Council, 26
Allies, 12
  effect of, on Western Europe, 26
  recognition of East Germany and, 66
  unification of West Berlin by, 31
America. *See* United States
Anhalter station, 100
Atlantic Alliance
  challenges to, 46
  Soviet perception of, 72
Austria, 105
Autobahn, 88

Balkan Pact, 72
Baltic, 72
Bastogne (Belgium), 39
Baumann, Karl-Hermann, 110
Beijing (China), 67
Belgium, 14, 89
Beria, Lavrenty
  execution of, 34, 61
  reduction of tensions with the West
    and, 59
Berlin
  bombing of, 114
  comparison of East and West, 97–98
  crime in, 124
  crisis, beginning of, 73
  as cultural center, 107–108
  direct East-West conflict in, 25
  immigration to, 122–24
  industrial base of, 119–20
  insecurities in, 121–22
  as mediator in Europe, 126
  Nazism and, 114
  reunification of, 21
  significance of, 25
  solidarity and, 122
  unification, immediate reaction to,
    98
  see also East Berlin; West Berlin
Berlin: The Wall Is Not Forever (Eleanor
  Lansing Dulles), 12
Berlin Wall

cosmopolitan crowd at fall of, 94
  logical development of postwar
    European politics, 81
  memorials along, 20
  peaceful solution to mass exodus, 36
  recognition of Democratic Republic
    and, 62
  separation of ideologies by, 24
  Soviet political strength and, 30
  symbolism of, 29
  tensions eased by, 28
  Ulbricht and, 69
Bismarck, Otto von, 110
Blockade: Berlin and the Cold War
  (Morris), 14–15
Bonn (Germany), 71, 73, 75
Brandenburg, 120
Brandenburgerplatz, 91
Brandenburg Gate, 97, 104
Brandt, Willy, 26, 116
Braunschweig (Germany), 89
British Broadcasting Corporation
  (BBC), 96

Camp David, 66
Canada, 14
Castro, Fidel, 16
Central Europe, 72
Charlottenburg (Germany), 81
Checkpoint Charlie, 100
Christian Democrats, 106, 107, 117
Churchill, Winston, 13
Church of Remembrance, 93
Civil Defense, 42–43, 80
Clay, Lucius, 26, 29
Cold War, 13–14
  importance of Berlin in, 24
  events of, 19
Cologne (Germany), 121
Cominform, 32–33
"Committee to Save the
  Ampelmannchen," 113
communism
  Berlin's symbolic significance to, 24
  Eastern Europe, controlled by, 32
  Third World nations and, 78
  worldwide threat of, 38
Communist Information Bureau,
  32–33
Congo, 78

136

Cooper, Belinda, 112
Craig, Campbell
  on Berlin's symbolic significance, 24
  on Kennedy's response to the
    creation of the wall, 18–19
Cuba, 36, 78
Cuban Missile Crisis, 19
cultural centers
  Cologne, 121
  Dusseldorf, 109
Czechoslovakia, 19, 53, 72

de Gaulle, Charles
  fear of nuclear war, 52
  meeting with Khrushchev, 75
Denmark, 14
Diepgen, Eberhard, 105
Dijk, Ruud van, 58
Dulles, Eleanor Lansing, 12
Dulles, John Foster, 52, 73
Du Quenoy, Paul, 30
Dusseldorf (Germany), 109

East Berlin, 13
  changes after reunification, 112–13
  escapes from, 19–20
  suicides of mayors of, 100
East German People's Police, 61
East German Socialist Unity Party
  (SED), 58
East Germany, 13, 72
  appropriation of aid by, 60
  conflict with Soviet leadership, 55
  difficulty with viability of, 35
  establishment of socialism in, 58
  fear of collapse of, 53
  identity of, 116
  justification for existence of, 58–59
  loss of industrial complex, 56
  political manipulation of the Soviet
    Union by, 59
  reaction to normal Western living,
    103–104
  resistance to change, 113–14
  showpiece of Socialist success, 14, 56
economy, 21
  budget cuts, 122
  centers of trade, 121
  East German monetary value, 92
  high-tech industry in, 109–11
  modern, 108–109, 112, 119
  optimism over, 92
  poverty and, 123
  service-based, 120–21
  tourism and, 118
Eisenhower, Dwight D., 15
  meeting at Camp David, 66, 75
  negotiations with Soviets, 27–28
England. *See* Great Britain

European Defense Community, 70
European Union (EU), 110

Fanfani, Amintore, 51
Fechter, Peter, 19–20
Federal Constitutional Court, 109
Federal Crime Agency, 109
Federal Republic of Germany, 13, 70
  see also West Germany
Fifth Congress of the SED, 64
Foster, Norman, 106
France, 89
  Algeria and, 52
  as Allied partner, 12–14, 25
  communism and, 32–33
  German reunification and, 52
  Ulbricht and, 66
  West German recovery and, 56
Frankfurt (Germany)
  Bundesbank (Central Bank) in, 109
  financial center, 120–21
Freie Universitat (Berlin), 17
Friedrechstrasse, 101
Fugmann-Heesing, Annette
  budget cuts and, 122
  political corruption and, 120
Fulbright, James William, 81

Gedankniskirchen. *See* Church of
  Remembrance
General Electric, 110
General Watson (American
  commander, Berlin), 18
Geneva (Switzerland), 28
German Defense Ministry, 109
German Democratic Republic (GDR)
  control of, 13
  as showcase of socialism, 56
  Socialist Unity Party and, 15
  U.S. recognition and, 81
  see also East Germany
German Parliament, 106
German Unification Day, 105
Germany
  capital of, 25
  division of, 12–13
  European security and, 74
  fear of power, 125
  foreign fears of unification, 99
  invasion of, by Soviet Union, 56
  as leading power in Europe, 109
  politics after unification of, 106–107
  reaction of, to Red Army, 56
  rearmament of, 58
  reunification of, 52
  tensions between East and West, 114
  visa requirements and, 13
  xenophobic atmosphere of, 112
  see also East Germany; West

Germany; *specific cities*
Glass, Andrew J., 104
Goethe, Johann, 101
Gorbachev, Mikhail, 58
government
  decentralization of, 125
  social needs and, 106
Great Britain
  as Allied partner, 12–13, 25
  conferences and, 66
  fear of nuclear war and, 27
  reaction of, to Soviet proposal to
    unify Berlin, 73
  West German reunification and, 52,
    56
Greece, 32
Green Party, 106, 118
Grotewohl, Otto, 58

Hamburg (Germany), 88, 109, 121
Hanover (Germany), 121
Harrison, Hope M., 55
Herrnstadt, Rudolf, 62
Herter, Christian A., 75
*History in Dispute Encyclopedia: The Cold
  War* (Du Quenoy), 30
Hitler's bunker, 91, 100
Honecker, Erich, 17, 99–100
Hope, Christopher, 96
Hungary, 105
  uprising of, 15, 64

IBM, 110
Iceland, 14
immigration
  elite professionals and, 35, 79
  Khrushchev and, 67
  number of people leaving, 84
  Ulbricht and, 17, 55
Iran, 31
"Iron Curtain," 13
Italy, 14
  communism and, 33
  nuclear war and, 51

Jewish Community Center, 100

Kaiser Wilhelm Memorial Church, 98
Kant Strasse, 102
Karlsruhe (Germany), 109
Kempenski Adlon. *See* Adlon
Kempinski Eck, 100
Kennedy, John F., 37, 67–68
  Bay of Pigs and, 16
  determination of, to strengthen West
    Berlin, 80
  initial reaction to Berlin Wall, 18, 84
  Khrushchev and, 28
  speech on Berlin crisis, 37–48

Soviet peace treaty and, 79
Khrushchev, Nikita S., 14, 49
  attempt to split Western solidarity,
    74
  Berlin as free city and, 73
  Camp David meeting and, 75
  challenge to leadership of, 64
  Communist takeover of Western
    Germany and, 71–72
  first ultimatum to U.S., 15, 27, 36
  French fears and, 75–76
  meeting with Eisenhower, 66
  "New Course" and, 34
  peace treaty with West and, 49
  reduction of tensions with West and,
    59
  second ultimatum to U.S., 68, 79
  on socialist economies dependence
    on the West, 53
  speech on Berlin, 49–53
  superiority of socialism and, 30
  threat to deny access to West Berlin,
    52
  Ubricht's unilateral actions and, 67
  value of East Berlin to, 35, 62–63
Kirste, Burkhard, 17–18
Kohl, Helmut
  German reunification and, 106
  tightening of asylum laws by, 123
Korea, 46
Kornblum, John, 109
Kosovo, 106
Kurfurstendamm, 92, 98
Kvitsinsky, Yuli, 68

Lafontaine, Oskar, 107
Laos, 36
Leipzig (Germany), 121
Luxembourg, 14

Macmillan, Harold, 51
  four-power summit and, 28
  view of Khrushchev, 74
Malenkov, Georgy, 34
  reduction of tensions with West and,
    59
  Soviet troops in East Germany and,
    61
Mansfield, Michael Joseph, 81
Marshall, George C., 13, 26
Marshall Plan, 13, 32
Martin Luther Strasse, 102
Marx, Karl, 62
McCloy, John J., 50
Mikoyan, Anastas, 63
Molotov, Vyacheslav, 31
Morris, Eric, 14, 15, 70
Munich (Germany), 109, 121
Murphy, Robert D., 26

Naimark, Norman, 56
National Committee for Free
   Germany, 58
Nazism, 114
neo-Nazis, 105, 123
Netherlands, 14
Neues Deutschland (newspaper), 62
"New Course," 59
   purpose of, 34
   standard of living in East Germany
      and, 60
Nokia, 110
North Atlantic Treaty Organization
   (NATO), 14, 37–38
   East Germany and, 75
   negotiations with Soviets, 27
   proposed nonaggression treaty with
      Warsaw Pact, 74
Norway, 14
November 11, 1989, 88
nuclear war
   Berlin Wall and, 82–83
   bluff by Soviets, 15
   impossibility of, 51–52
   U.S. monopoly on weapons for, 27
   U.S. preparations for, 42–43

Olympics (2000), 120
One, Two, Three (movie), 105
Opera House, 98
"Ossies" (foreigners), 99, 102–103

Paris (France), 28, 75
Party of Democratic Socialism (PDS)
   popular support of, 107
   success of, 117
Pervukhin, Mikhail, 68–69
Pieck, Wilhelm, 58
Poland, 53, 64, 72, 104
Politburo, 62
politics
   corruption of, 120
   parties, 117–118
   social needs and, 106
Portugal, 14
Potsdam (Germany), 72
Potsdamer Platz, 91, 100
Powers, Gary, 77
President Kennedy: Profile of Power
   (Reeves), 84
Prussia, 25

Ramos, Andreas, 88
Rapacki Plan, 72
Reeves, Richard, 84
Reichstag, 105, 106
Romanian Gypsies, 123
"Rose" (code name for Berlin Wall),
   36, 69

Russia. *See* Soviet Union
Ryback, Timothy W., 19–20

Schabowski, Gunter, 20
Schirdewan, Karl, 64
Schmidt, Helmut, 106
Schroder, Gerhard, 106
Schumacher, Kurt, 33
Schumann, Conrad, 19
Shanghai (China), 108
Siemens AG, 110
Social Democrats, 106
Socialist Unity Party, 15
social systems
   challenges to, 122
   social needs and, 106
   structure of, 21
Southeast Asia, 38
Soviet Occupation of Germany, The
   (Naimark), 56
Soviet Union, 25
   Chinese relations with, 67
   commitment to East Germany,
      64–65
   concern over harsh East German
      politics, 65–66
   East German leadership and, 55
   East German refugee problem and,
      63
   foreign policy of, 57, 62, 78
   Greek uprising and, 31–32
   Kennedy's speech on Berlin and, 50
   leadership struggle after Stalin, 14
   military-base rights and, 31
   NATO and, 73
   nonaggression treaty and, 74–75
   nuclear weapons and, 15–16
   power struggle in, 64
   suppression of East German
      uprising, 61
   treatment of Germany after World
      War II, 31, 56
   Western recognition of Democratic
      Republic and, 82
Spain, 89
Stalin, Joseph, 13
   blockade of Berlin by, 26, 33–34
   death of, 14
   demilitarization and, 72
   Soviet expansion and, 30–31
   unification of Germany and, 33,
      57–58
Stalingrad (Russia), 39
Stasi (East German secret police), 105
Sweden, 89

Tegel Airport, 105
Third Reich, 25, 104
Tito, Josip, 31

Trabants (cars), 89, 98
Truman, Harry S., 13
  Berlin airlift and, 26–27
  Communist expansion and, 32
  Truman Doctrine, 32
Turkey, 31
Twentieth Party Congress, 64

U-2 incident, 28, 36, 77
U-Bahn, 98
Ulbricht, Walter, 15, 34–35, 49, 58, 66
  Beria and, 62
  campaign of, against West German
    citizens, 81
  manipulation of Khrushchev by, 55
  "New Course" and, 60
  production quotas and, 60–61
  restriction of access to West Berlin
    by, 65–66
  role of, in building the wall, 17
  Sino-Soviet conflict and, 67
  Soviet aid and, 57
  unilateral decisions by, 55, 78
  unified Berlin and, 17
Union of Soviet Socialist Republics
  (USSR). *See* Soviet Union
United Kingdom, 14
United Nations, 78, 81
United States
  as Allied partner, 12–13, 25
  budgetary concerns, 43–44
  commitment to peace in Berlin,
    44–46
  embassy rebuilding, 109
  Germany's reunification and, 52
  NATO and, 14
  as nuclear monopoly, 27
  rebuilding of West Germany and, 56
  U-2 incident and, 77
Unter Den Linden, 101, 104

Vienna (Austria), 28, 68, 79

Vietnam War, 19

Warsaw Pact, 105
  Berlin Crisis and, 68
  nonaggression treaty with NATO,
    74–75
  secret meeting of, 81
  signing of, 15
Weimar Republic, 114
Weissensee Jewish cemetery, 105
"Wessies" (West Berliners), 99
West Berlin, 12–13
  airlift for, 13–14
  blockade of, 57
  cultural chauvinism and, 115
  disrespect for power and privilege in,
    97
  economic concerns, 99
  mayor of, 117
  as symbol of freedom, 39
  as threat to Soviet empire and
    Eastern Europe, 71
  underground escape system in, 19
West Germany, 12, 72
  decentralized structure of, 109
  discrimination against East Germans
    by, 116–17
  NATO and, 15
  recovery of, 56–57
Westin Grand (hotel), 105
Wettig, Gerhard, 58
Wiesbaden (Germany), 109
Wilhelmstrasse, 100
Winged Victory (statue), 91
World War II, 12
  destruction of Berlin during, 114
  German-Soviet relations and, 56
  signs of, in Berlin, 100–101

Yugoslavia, 31–32

Zaisser, Wilhelm, 62